Fast Favorites under Pressure

Meredith Laurence

Photography by Jessica Walker

Walah!, LLC Publishers
Philadelphia

First Edition

Published in the United States by Walah!, LLC/Publishers

walah@me.com

Library of Congress Cataloging-in-Publication Data

    Laurence, Meredith, author.
       Fast favorites under pressure / Meredith Laurence ;
    photography by Jessica Walker. -- First edition.
       pages cm
       Includes index.
       ISBN 978-0-9827540-2-3

       1. Pressure cooking. 2. Cookbooks.   I. Title.

   TX840.P7L384 2016   641.5'87
                       QBI16-600015

Printed in USA

Book design by Janis Boehm
www.bound-determined.com

Photography by Jessica Walker
www.jessicawalkerphotography.com

Food styling by Bonne Di Tomo, Lisa Ventura and Lynn Willis

About this Book

The recipes in this cookbook are accessible to everyone. You'll find basic recipes here for the newcomer, as well as slightly more challenging recipes for those who want to take their pressure-cooking to the next level. I believe that every recipe in this book is something anyone can make, but I've marked those recipes that are *really* easy with a "Super Easy" stamp.

In addition, I want to make sure that there are lots of options for all kinds of cooks so I included a vegetarian main dishes section, and scattered a few more vegetarian recipes throughout the other sections of the book. All these recipes are marked with a "Vegetarian" stamp so you can quickly identify them. Finally, I want you to know what *my* favorite recipes from the book are and I've marked those as "BJC Fav's".

The recipes in this book were tested with various 4-quart electric pressure cookers. If you are using a stovetop pressure cooker, if you are cooking at a high altitude, or if you are interested in converting other recipes that you have made with traditional methods take a look at the section **Converting Recipes** on page 14.

Table of Contents

★ Blue Jean Chef Favorites   ■ Super Easy Recipes   ▼ Vegetarian

Table of Contents

★ Blue Jean Chef Favorites   ■ Super Easy Recipes   ▼ Vegetarian

Grains and Beans

Vegetable Side Dishes

Desserts

About the Author

Meredith Laurence, the Blue Jean Chef, has worked in numerous capacities and settings in the food world. After graduating from the New England Culinary Institute, she first honed her skills in two Michelin-rated restaurants in Les-Baux-de-Provence, France. She then went on to work as a line cook at Zuni Café in San Francisco and at Café Rouge in Berkeley, California.

Meredith set out on a different culinary path when she returned to teach at the New England Culinary Institute in Vermont, instructing professional culinary students during the day and home cooks in the evenings. Having found her real passion for teaching home cooks, she moved back to San Francisco to teach and manage at two HomeChef cooking schools. At the same time, Meredith worked in the world of food and product consulting at the Center for Culinary Development, where she acquired an expertise in creating and testing recipes. She now works as the Blue Jean Chef on live television doing on air cooking demonstrations, giving QVC customers advice on cooking and equipping their kitchens.

As the Blue Jean Chef, Meredith's belief is that being comfortable in the kitchen is key to successful and enjoyable cooking. How comfortable? Well, as comfortable as you would be in your favorte jeans, relaxing with friends.

Meredith's first book, *Blue Jean Chef: Comfortable in the Kitchen*, received rave reviews and helped home cooks broaden their repertoire and become more versatile with a variety of cooking techniques in the kitchen.

Meredith's next two cookbooks, *Blue Jean Chef: Comfortable Under Pressure* and *Delicious Under Pressure*, were both best-sellers and helped home cooks take pressure-cooking to a new level with creative recipes and clear instruction using the time-saving method of pressure-cooking.

In addition to her cookbook writing and appearances on television, Meredith also writes and appears in a web-series called *The Basics*, which can be seen on YouTube (www.youtube.com/bluejeanchef). *The Basics* takes viewers through a series of easy cooking techniques and recipes, empowering even the most novice cook.

For more information on Meredith, please visit www.bluejeanchef.com.

Introduction

My mother always used to tell me that the kitchen appliances we are most likely to use are the ones that we keep on our counter-top. This is so true! If you have to run to the basement or garage to retrieve your microwave, toaster oven, or pressure cooker, you're much less likely to use it. Indeed, even if you have to rummage around a lower cabinet to pull the appliance out, you're less likely to use it to make dinner. It speaks volumes about our need for convenience, or lack of precious time as a society, but it's true.

It's that same need for convenience that makes us want to use pressure cookers. Cooking under pressure is a great way to put delicious meals on the table in one third of the time it would take to create the same meal on the stovetop or in the oven. Imagine having two thirds of your cooking time given back to you to do with as you wish – clean up the kitchen, lay the table, complete another household chore or just relax for a minute!

So how to reconcile these two issues – needing an efficient appliance AND making sure you use it regularly? Well, it's not rocket science. A smaller pressure cooker offers you the best of both worlds – you can create the delicious meals in a short period of time AND with it's small footprint you can keep it on your counter so that you're sure to use it regularly.

Most recipes for pressure cookers are written for larger cookers, making big batches of food to feed 6 or more people. Lately, however, household sizes are getting smaller and smaller. The average household size in 2015 was just over 2 people. While it is certainly easy to make meals for a crowd and freeze the left-overs for a rainy day, sometimes it is nice to have the right sized recipe for the right sized cooker... a cooker that is sitting on your countertop. That's what this book is all about.

As the Blue Jean Chef, my goal is to get folks comfortable in the kitchen... as comfortable as you'd be in your favorite jeans. In this book, my goal is to make sure you are comfortable pressure-cooking and making delicious meals in no time. If this is your first venture into pressure-cooking, be sure to read the If You are Brand New to Pressure Cooking... section on page XXX. If you're more experienced, you might skip over that section and head to the General Tips for Pressure Cooking section on page XXX. No matter what your experience level, to get the most out of this book and its recipes, check out the Recipe Rules on page 18.

Let's jump in and get comfortable!

If You are Brand New to Pressure Cooking...

Pressure Cooker Basics

A pressure cooker is a cooking vessel with a lid that locks on and prevents steam from escaping. As a result, the steam builds up pressure in the pressure cooker – about 12 to 15 pounds per square inch of pressure (psi) – and the temperature inside the cooker increases. At sea level, water boils at 212º F before it is converted into steam, and it cannot get any hotter than that, regardless of the heat source below it. In a pressure cooker, with 15 psi of pressure added, water boils at 250º F before being converted into steam. That means that we are able to cook foods inside a pressure cooker at higher temperatures, and they are therefore finished sooner – in about one third of the time it would take to cook on a regular stovetop. The time saved by using a pressure cooker is obviously a huge benefit, but that is secondary to how your foods taste out of the pressure cooker.

In a pressure cooker, the lid is sealed onto the pot letting nothing escape, and the flavors of the foods have nowhere to go but to mingle with each other. With flavor infused throughout, soups, stews, chilies, everything is intensely flavorful. Cuts of meat that usually need a long cooking time in order to become tender are transformed into spoon-tender, succulent meals. Because the lid prevents steam from escaping, foods remain moist too. The results of pressure-cooking are juicy, tender, moist and flavorful meals. All of that in one-third of the time it would normally take. You can't beat that!

Health Benefits

There are also health benefits to pressure-cooking. The main cooking medium in pressure-cooking is liquid rather than fat. When pressure-cooking, you can choose to almost eliminate fats, creating lean meals. Vegetables can be steamed quickly, retaining their crunch, color and nutrients.

Energy Efficient

Because it saves time and cooks foods faster, pressure cookers use up less energy than traditional methods of cooking. Also, because the steam and heat are trapped in the pressure cooker, you will find that your kitchen remains cooler. I love this for the summer months. With a pressure cooker, you have the versatility to cook foods all year round that you might otherwise reserve just for the winter.

Safe and Easy to Use

Pressure-cooking is also safe and easy. Most recipes call for you to start by browning foods either in the cooker itself or on the stovetop. Then, you combine the food with at least one to one and a half cups of liquid (check your pressure cooker manual for the minimum liquid requirement), lock the lid in place and set a timer. Electric pressure cookers do all the monitoring of time and temperature for you, so all you have to do is wait for the time to expire. There are safety valves built in to control for any unplanned occurrence and the locks on the machines prevent you from making a mistake and opening the unit when there's pressure inside. The horror stories of pressure cookers blowing up are truly tales of the past.

One of my favorite aspects of pressure-cooking is waiting for the timer to ring. I always have enough time to clean up the kitchen and set the table, which means that after dinner, I only have one pot and a few plates to clean.

Combining Pressure-Cooking with Other Cooking Techniques

Pressure-cooking can be your sole cooking method, or it can just speed up the process of making a meal combined with a different cooking technique. Ribs, for example, can be cooked in the pressure cooker and then popped onto the grill and brushed with BBQ sauce with an excellent result. Hams can be cooked in the pressure cooker and then glazed under the broiler for easy and beautiful browning.

Browning First

For visual appeal as well as for flavor, it's important to brown your foods either before pressure-cooking, or after the food has been cooked. Many electric pressure cookers now have BROWN settings, which will allow you to sear foods before you add the liquid required for cooking. If your electric pressure cooker does not have a BROWN setting, you can often use one of the pre-programmed buttons in order to brown. Turning the pre-programmed button on will engage the bottom element and as long as you don't put the lid on, you can brown in the pot. Alternatively, you can simply brown the foods on the stovetop in a skillet first, add the liquid to the skillet to deglaze the pan and scrape up any brown bits that have formed on the bottom from searing the meat, and pour the entire thing into the pressure cooker along with the remaining ingredients. It's a small step that does take a little time, but it is important to the final result.

Releasing Pressure

There are two ways to release the pressure in a pressure cooker. The first way is called the *natural release method.* This involves simply turning your electric pressure cooker off. The temperature will slowly decrease in the cooker and the pressure will come back to normal. Understand that a natural pressure release can take as long as fifteen minutes, so account for that time in your meal planning. Use the natural release method for meats in order to obtain the most tender results, for beans whose skins tend to burst otherwise, and for dishes with a lot of liquid where the liquid might spit out of the pressure release valve.

The alternative method to release the pressure in a pressure cooker is called the *quick-release method.* Electric pressure cookers have a release valve that you can turn to release the pressure manually. Steam will escape out of the valve until the pressure has returned to normal. Use the quick-release method for foods that are easily over-cooked, like grains, seafood or vegetables.

Converting Recipes

Converting From Traditional Recipes

Converting traditional recipes into pressure cooker recipes is easy. First step is to make sure you have one to one and a half cups of liquid (check your pressure cooker manual for the minimum liquid requirement) included in the recipe. There is very little evaporation during pressure-cooking, so you don't want a lot of liquid, but you do need the minimum required to steam and build the pressure. The next step is to simply cook the dish for one third of the time called for in the original recipe. Finally, use the appropriate release method for whatever it is you are cooking based on the **Releasing Pressure** explanation section above.

Converting From Slow Cooker Recipes

Converting slow cooker recipes into pressure cooker recipes is also easy. There is very little evaporation from either slow cookers or pressure cookers, so they tend to have similar liquid quantities. Make sure the recipe has at least one to one and a half cups of liquid (check your pressure cooker manual for the minimum liquid requirement) and then use the cooking charts on page XXX or a similar recipe from the book to determine the cooking time for your meal.

Converting to Stovetop Pressure Cookers

Stovetop pressure cookers get to pressure a little faster than electric pressure cookers and also drop their pressure a little faster than electric pressure cookers. Because of this, the actual cooking time of foods in a stovetop pressure cooker is shorter than when using an electric pressure cooker. However, stovetop pressure cookers often reach a higher pressure level than electric pressure cookers, so it almost evens out. You won't find much difference in the timing for many recipes, but if you are cooking big pieces of meat, beans or grains, reduce the cooking time by a couple of minutes for stovetop cookers.

Converting to Larger Pressure Cookers

The recipes in this book are easy to increase if you're cooking for a crowd and have a bigger pressure cooker. Just multiply all the ingredients by 1.5 or 2 times, but keep the cooking time the same. It may take longer for the cooker to come to pressure, since it takes longer to bring more food to a boil, but the cooking time should be the same.

Converting for High Altitudes

Anyone cooking at a high altitude knows that water boils at a lower temperature because of the decreased atmospheric pressure. This affects the pressure inside a pressure cooker as well. So, when using a pressure cooker at higher altitudes, increase the cooking time by 5% for every 1000 feet over 2000 feet above sea level.

General Tips for Pressure-Cooking

Preparing to pressure cook

● Always use at least one to one and a half cups of liquid (or the minimum amount of liquid suggested by your pressure cooker manufacturer). Unfortunately, this does NOT include canned tomatoes or prepared sauces like BBQ sauce. The liquid required needs to be watery, like juice, wine, stock, or water.

● Never fill your pressure cooker more than two-thirds full.

● For ingredients that foam or expand in the pressure cooker – like pasta, beans, grains, legumes and some fruit – be sure to only fill the cooker half full. It is also prudent to add a little oil to the cooker when cooking these ingredients to help prevent foaming.

● Check the gasket of your pressure cooker before each use, to make sure that it is clean and properly in place. The gasket can hold on to odors from cooking. Try washing it in a vinegar-water solution to keep it odor free.

● If you're in a rush and you still want to brown the meat before pressure-cooking, double up and use a second skillet on the stovetop as well as the pressure cooker to sear the meat. You'll get twice as much meat browned in the same amount of time.

● If your cooker does not have a specific "brown" setting, just turn the cooker on and do not cover with the lid. The element at the bottom of the cooker will engage and heat up and you'll be able to brown right in the cooker.

Setting and building the pressure

● 95% of all pressure cooker recipes call for HIGH pressure. If your pressure cooker doesn't have low-medium-high settings for pressure, you probably only have the high setting. Because so many cookers only have the high setting, you'll find all the recipes in this book use high pressure.

● Some pressure cookers use the metric measure of kilopascals (kPa) as the unit of pressure, rather than pounds per square inch (psi). HIGH pressure is usually 12 to 15 psi, which would be roughly 80 to 100 kPa. To convert from kPa to psi, multiply the number of kPa by 0.15.

● Remember that it takes time for the pressure cooker to build the pressure inside. Depending on what and how much food you are cooking, that time can be as much as fifteen minutes. Try to account for that time the same way you would account for the time it takes for your oven to pre-heat.

● If your pressure cooker doesn't seem to be coming to pressure it might be because you don't have enough liquid inside. Open it up and add more liquid before trying again.

● If you find that steam is escaping from around the rim of your pressure cooker, or through the pressure release valve, check that the valve is closed and give the lid a firm push down. Pushing down on the lid helps the gasket form a seal around the rim of the pressure cooker and the cooker should almost immediately stop releasing steam and come to pressure. I do this almost every time

I use a pressure cooker to ensure accurate timing of the recipe. Once the machine has come to pressure, I walk away and let it do the rest of the work.

Releasing the pressure

● A natural release can take longer than you think it should, depending on what and how much food you have inside the cooker. My rule of thumb is to allow a natural release for fifteen minutes. After that, I will release any residual pressure with the quick-release method without any negative effects.

● If the steam releasing from your pressure cooker during a quick-release starts to spit and sputter liquid, close the valve and let the pressure drop naturally. You can also hold a kitchen towel above the pressure release valve to stop any splattering from messing up your cabinets.

● Be careful opening the lid of the pressure cooker. Even though the pressure will have dropped, the food inside will still be very hot and steam will be released.

Finishing touches

● Because you need liquid to create the steam needed to build pressure, you never thicken the sauce before cooking. Instead, thicken sauces once the cooking procedure is over. You can do this by whisking in flour, adding a beurre manié (equal parts soft butter and flour mixed together), stirring in a slurry (cornstarch dissolved in a tablespoon of water), or by adding potato flakes or cornmeal. Whatever you add, make sure you bring the liquid back to a simmer in order to thicken it.

● Let the food cool for at least 5 minutes before serving it. Foods become very hot in a pressure cooker and not only are they likely to burn you if you eat them too quickly, but the flavors need a little time to blend and settle before serving.

● Invest in accessories for your pressure cooker. It will expand your repertoire.

  ● A rack that fits inside your pressure cooker is very important to have. I have two small racks about 5-inches long by 4-inches wide. These can be used in any combination to fit most pressure cookers.

  ● A small 7-inch cake pan will fit inside most pressure cookers. You'll need this to cook all the bread puddings and cheesecakes.

  ● A steamer basket is nice to have in a pressure cooker for steaming vegetables among other things.

● Rarely, but on occasion, you might experience a "blow out" with your pressure cooker. This is not a sign of a faulty cooker, but is in fact a safety mechanism. A "blow out" is when the steam will suddenly be released from the cooker usually from the side of the lid. It occurs when too much pressure has built up in the cooker. Let the pressure drop completely, open the lid, make sure all the valves are clean and try your recipe again.

Recipe Rules

In every cooking class I've ever taught, I try to set people up for success by setting some ground rules. Sounds strict, but it really isn't. I prefer to think of these rules as helpful hints.

First rule – read the recipe from start to finish before you begin cooking. This is critical in order to know if you have all the ingredients, as well as if you have enough time to complete the recipe. Don't forget to account for the time it takes to come to pressure, as well as the time it takes to release the pressure naturally.

Second rule – buy the very best ingredients you can. A finished dish can only taste as good as its ingredients.

Third rule – do your *mise en place.* This means do all your prep work first. Chop what needs to be chopped. Measure what needs to be measured. This makes cooking much less stressful and more relaxing. Of course, you can start a step of the recipe in the middle of doing your *mise en place* if that first step in the recipe requires some time. You'll know this because you will have read the recipe all the way through first!

Fourth rule – taste your food before you take it to the table. You'd be surprised how many people forget this step, but it's really important. You should always take a few seconds to taste the food and re-season it if necessary.

Specifics about Ingredients

- **Tomatoes.** I prefer to use canned whole tomatoes and then chop or crush them by hand. I think they taste better than canned diced or crushed tomatoes. So, when you see "1 (28-ounce) can tomatoes, chopped", that means a can of whole tomatoes, chopped by hand. (Of course, you can substitute canned diced tomatoes if you want or need to.) Unless other wise specified, add everything that comes in the can of tomatoes – tomatoes and their juice – to the recipe. Remember that tomatoes do not count as the minimum liquid required in order to build the pressure.

- **Onions, Garlic and Carrots.** Unless you enjoy eating the skin and peels of these vegetables, assume that they should always be peeled.

- **Potatoes.** I specify whether or not to peel the potatoes before using them in the recipes. If it doesn't say "peeled" that means wash the potatoes, but leave the skins on.

- **Peppers.** People have different tastes and capacities to handle spicy foods. Similarly, chili peppers have very different levels of spiciness, even within the same type of pepper. If you like spicy foods, feel free to leave the seeds in the peppers. If you do not like spicy foods, always seed the peppers before incorporating them into the recipe. I don't say one way or another what to do, but leave the decision up to you.

- **Wine.** Unless otherwise specified, use dry wines in the recipes rather than sweet wines. Whatever you do, do not use cooking wine, which is filled with sodium and does not add any good flavors to your finished dish.

- **Substitution for Wine.** If you don't want to cook with wine for whatever reason, there are a number of substitutions you can make. Just think about what will add the best flavor to your finished dish. For red wine, try beef, chicken or rich vegetable stock, cranberry, pomegranate or red grape juice, or some red wine vinegar. For white wine, try chicken or vegetable stock, white grape or apple juice, or some white wine vinegar or lemon juice.

- **Good quality stock and other ingredients.** Sometimes you will see instruction to use "good quality stock" rather than just stock, or "Parmigiano-Reggiano cheese" rather than just Parmesan cheese. While I strongly recommend using the very best ingredients all the time, sometimes an ingredient has extra importance in a recipe and absolutely must be of the highest quality. If you see "good quality", then you'll know that you can't substitute an inferior ingredient in its place and expect the same excellent results.

I may call them rules, but all of these points are just to set you off on the right path!

If you would like to learn more about pressure-cooking, or would like more recipes for your pressure cooker and other cooking tools, please visit me at www.bluejeanchef.com.

Soups
and
Chilies

Tortilla Soup
Cream of Broccoli Soup
Lentil Soup with Ham and Kale
Chicken and Corn Chowder
Italian Wedding Soup
Avglolemono with Chicken and Rice
Cauliflower Cheddar Soup
Tuscan Bean Soup with Tomatoes and Spinach
Manhattan Clam Chowder
Split Pea and Ham Soup
Quinoa Chili with Kidney Beans and Corn
Black Bean and Mushroom Chili
Chipotle Chickpea Chicken Chili
Chili con Carne
Chile Verde

Tortilla Soup

This soup is a favorite of mine. I love Mexican flavors and this soup is like a burrito in a bowl minus the rice. I don't know about you, but I don't often have leftover or stale tortilla chips to use up in this soup, but you don't have to twist my arm to buy a new bag either!

Serves
4 to 6

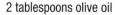

Cooking Time
8 Minutes

Release Method
Quick-release

2 tablespoons olive oil

1 onion, finely diced

2 cloves garlic, minced

1 Jalapeño pepper, minced or sliced into rings

1 red bell pepper, chopped

1 tablespoon chili powder

1 teaspoon ground cumin

1 (28-ounce) can fire-roasted tomatoes, diced

3 cups good quality or homemade unsalted chicken stock

1 (15-ounce) can black beans, drained and rinsed

1 (15-ounce) can red kidney beans, drained and rinsed

2 boneless skinless chicken breasts, cut in half

salt and freshly ground black pepper

4 cups (about 6 ounces) corn tortilla chips, broken into pieces

1 avocado, peeled and sliced

½ cup fresh cilantro leaves

½ cup grated Cheddar cheese

1. Pre-heat the pressure cooker using the BROWN setting.

2. Add the olive oil and sauté the onion until it starts to soften – about 5 minutes. Add the garlic, Jalapeño pepper, red pepper and spices, and cook for another minute or two. Add the tomatoes, chicken stock, beans and chicken breasts, submerging the chicken under the liquid. Lock the lid in place.

3. Pressure cook on HIGH for 8 minutes.

4. Release the pressure using the QUICK-RELEASE method and carefully remove the lid. Remove the chicken to a side plate and when cool enough to touch, shred the chicken with two forks into small pieces.

5. Return the chicken to the soup and season to taste with salt and freshly ground black pepper. Place some tortilla chips into each bowl and ladle the soup on top. Garnish with avocado, cilantro and Cheddar cheese.

Substitution

You can use dried beans in this recipe if you prefer. Just cook ½ cup of each bean together first, covered in water on HIGH pressure for 5 minutes. Let the pressure drop naturally, drain the beans and then proceed with the recipe from the beginning.

Cream of Broccoli Soup

I tried to dress this soup up by adding some beans and some bacon, but I kept coming back to how nice it is sometimes to just keep things simple. This is a quick, easy and simply delicious soup.

Serves
4 to 6

Cooking Time
4 Minutes

Release Method
Quick-release

1 tablespoon olive oil

1 onion, chopped (1 cup)

1 teaspoon dried thyme leaves

10 cups of broccoli, stems sliced and florets broken into pieces
(about 1½ to 2 heads)

salt and freshly ground black pepper

3 cups water or vegetable stock

½ cup heavy cream

chopped fresh chives, for garnish

1. Pre-heat the pressure cooker using the BROWN setting.

2. Add the oil, onion and thyme. Cook for 4 to 5 minutes, stirring occasionally. Add the broccoli and season with salt and pepper. Pour in the water or stock and lock the lid in place.

3. Pressure cook on HIGH for 4 minutes.

4. Reduce the pressure with QUICK-RELEASE method and carefully remove the lid. Purée the soup in batches using a blender (remembering not to fill the blender more than half full with the hot mixture) or an immersion blender. Return the soup to the cooker while it is still hot and stir in the heavy cream. Season the soup again to taste with salt and pepper. Sprinkle the chives on top and serve.

Want to add a little interest? Garnish this with cooked chopped bacon and a dollop of sour cream.

Lentil Soup with Ham and Kale

This is a hearty soup that can easily be a meal unto itself. It's full of protein and nutrients, but its best feature is its flavor! The French green lentils hold their shape in this soup. If you'd prefer the soup thicker and softer, use regular lentils.

Serves
4

Cooking Time
8 Minutes

Release Method
Quick-release

1 tablespoon olive oil

½ onion, finely chopped (about ½ cup)

1 carrot, finely chopped

1 rib celery, finely chopped

4 ounces ham, diced (about ¾ cup)

1 clove garlic, minced

½ teaspoon dried thyme

¼ teaspoon dried rosemary

¼ teaspoon crushed red pepper flakes

4 cups chicken stock

1 cup dried French green (de Puy) lentils

4 cups packed cups chopped curly leaf kale

1 teaspoon salt

freshly ground black pepper

1. Pre-heat the pressure cooker using the BROWN setting.

2. Add the olive oil and cook the onion, carrot and celery until the vegetables start to soften – about 4 to 5 minutes. Add the diced ham, garlic, thyme, rosemary and red pepper flakes and cook for another minute. Add the chicken stock and lentils, and stir in the chopped kale. Season with salt and pepper and lock the lid in place.

3. Pressure cook on HIGH for 8 minutes.

4. Release the pressure using the QUICK-RELEASE method and carefully remove the lid.

5. Season again to taste and serve.

If you have a ham bone in your fridge or freezer, now's the time to use it! Let this soup cook with the ham bone for extra flavor.

Chicken and Corn Chowder

This is a great soup to have at the end of the summer when corn is still in season and you're looking forward to the fall. But, don't fret if you're craving corn chowder outside of corn season – you can use frozen kernels for this just as easily.

Serves
4 to 6

Cooking Time
8 Minutes

Release Method
Quick-release

2 tablespoons olive oil

1 onion, finely diced

3 ribs of celery, finely diced

1 red bell pepper, finely diced

2 cloves garlic, minced

3 cups fresh corn kernels or
1-pound bag frozen corn kernels

1 teaspoon dried thyme leaves

⅛ teaspoon crushed red pepper flakes

2 teaspoons salt

freshly ground black pepper

3 cups chicken stock

2 large chicken breasts, on the bone but skin removed

1 tablespoon flour

½ to 1 cup heavy cream

¼ cup sliced scallions

1. Pre-heat the pressure cooker using the BROWN setting.

2. Add the oil and sauté the onion and celery for 3 to 4 minutes. Add the red pepper, garlic, corn kernels, thyme, crushed red pepper flakes, salt and black pepper and mix well, cooking for another minute or two.

3. Add the chicken stock and chicken breasts, and make sure the chicken is submerged in the liquid. Lock the lid in place.

4. Pressure cook on HIGH for 8 minutes.

5. Release the pressure using the QUICK-RELEASE method and carefully remove the lid. Remove the chicken to a side plate and let it cool slightly so that you can shred the chicken with your fingers. While the chicken cools, purée 2 cups of the soup along with the flour using a blender or immersion blender. Return the puréed soup and the shredded chicken to the cooker and mix well.

6. Return the cooker to the BROWN setting, pour in the heavy cream , adding enough to give the soup the desired consistency. Season to taste with salt and pepper, and serve with chopped scallions on top.

Dress It Up

A nice way to give this soup a little more pizzazz is to make your own croutons to go on top. Cut a few slices of Italian or multi-grain bread into large cubes, toss with olive oil, salt and pepper and toast in a 350ºF oven for about 10 to 15 minutes, or until nicely browned. This is also really nice with oyster crackers.

Italian Wedding Soup

You might think that Italian Wedding Soup is what is served at Italian weddings, but in fact the soup's title is actually a reference to the perfect marriage between the green vegetables and the meat.

Serves
6 to 8

Cooking Time
10 Minutes

Release Method
Natural-release

Meatballs:

½ pound lean ground beef

¾ cup panko breadcrumbs

1 egg

½ cup grated Parmesan cheese

1 teaspoon Italian seasoning

1½ teaspoons dried parsley

½ teaspoon salt

¼ teaspoon black pepper

Soup:

2 tablespoons butter

1 tablespoon olive oil

1 onion, finely chopped

2 carrots, finely chopped

1 teaspoon Italian seasoning

½ teaspoon salt

¼ teaspoon black pepper

7 cups chicken stock

½ cup acini di pepe pasta

1 bunch escarole, washed and thickly shredded

grated Parmesan cheese

1. For the meatballs, combine all the meatball ingredients in a large bowl and mix well until everything is combined. Roll the meatball mixture into small balls, roughly 1 tablespoon of meat per meatball. Place the rolled meatballs into the freezer on a cookie sheet for at least 30 minutes.

2. Pre-heat the pressure cooker using the BROWN setting.

3. Add the butter and olive oil to the cooker and sauté the onions and carrots for five minutes, until the vegetables start to soften. Add the Italian seasoning, salt and pepper and pour in the chicken stock. Stir in the pasta and partially frozen meatballs and lock the lid in place.

4. Pressure cook on HIGH for 10 minutes.

5. Let the pressure drop NATURALLY for ten minutes, then release any residual pressure and carefully remove the lid. Let the soup sit for a couple of minutes and then spoon off any fat that rises to the surface. Stir in the shredded escarole to wilt and season with salt and pepper to taste. Serve in bowls with grated Parmesan cheese on top.

Avglolemono with Chicken and Rice

I had a Greek math teacher in high school who used to make Avglolemono for her young daughters at their request. It's like the Greek equivalent to chicken noodle soup, but it has rice instead of noodles, is thickened with egg and seasoned with lemon juice. I'm not sure if it has the healing powers of chicken noodle soup, but I know that it's incredibly satisfying.

Serves
4

Cooking Time
8 Minutes

Release Method
Quick-release

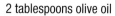

2 tablespoons olive oil

1 onion, finely diced (about 1 cup)

1 cup long-grain rice

4 cups good quality or homemade unsalted chicken stock

2 chicken breasts, on the bone, but skin removed

2 eggs, lightly beaten

1 lemon, zest and juice

salt and freshly ground black pepper, to taste

¼ cup fresh parsley leaves

1. Pre-heat the pressure cooker using the BROWN setting.

2. Add the olive oil and sauté the onion until it starts to soften – about 5 minutes. Add the rice, stir well and cook for another minute or two. Add the chicken stock and chicken breasts, submerging them under the liquid. Lock the lid in place.

3. Pressure cook on HIGH for 8 minutes.

4. Release the pressure using the QUICK-RELEASE method and carefully remove the lid. Remove the chicken to a side plate and when cool enough to touch, pull the meat from the bone and chop into small pieces.

5. While the chicken cools, whisk the eggs in a bowl until frothy. Whisking constantly, add the lemon juice to the eggs and then add a ladle full of the hot broth. Whisk this mixture back into the hot pressure cooker. The soup should thicken nicely. Stir the chopped chicken back into the soup and season to taste with salt and freshly ground black pepper. Serve with some lemon zest and a few parsley leaves on top.

This soup will continue to get thicker as it sits or if kept as leftovers. You can thin it out to the right consistency with more chicken stock or water.

Cauliflower Cheddar Soup

You'll want a good sharp Cheddar cheese for this soup to give it a pronounced flavor, so pick your favorite Cheddar and it's flavor will shine through.

Serves
4

Cooking Time
6 Minutes

Release Method
Quick-release

2 tablespoons butter

1 onion, chopped (1 cup)

1 clove garlic, smashed

1 teaspoon fresh thyme leaves

1 medium head of cauliflower, chopped

salt and freshly ground black pepper

2 cups chicken stock

2 cups grated sharp white Cheddar cheese

4 scallions, sliced on the bias

ground paprika or cayenne pepper, for garnish

1. Pre-heat the pressure cooker using the BROWN setting.

2. Add the butter, onion, garlic and thyme. Cook for 4 to 5 minutes, stirring occasionally. Add the cauliflower and season with salt and pepper. Pour in the chicken stock and lock the lid in place.

3. Pressure cook on HIGH for 6 minutes.

4. Release the pressure using the QUICK-RELEASE method and carefully remove the lid. Purée the soup in batches using a blender (remembering not to fill the blender more than half full with the hot mixture) or all at one time with an immersion blender. Return the soup to the cooker while it is still hot, add the cheese and stir until it has all melted. Season the soup again to taste with salt and pepper. Sprinkle the scallions and paprika on top and serve.

Don't feel like blending the soup? Give it a good stir with a wooden spoon and leave it chunky.

Tuscan Bean Soup
with Tomatoes and Spinach

This soup is one of my favorites. With the ciabatta on the bottom, the beans and the spinach it truly is a meal all to itself. Ciabatta translates as "slipper bread" because of it's elongated flat shape. It has a crispy crust and an airy texture inside that absorbs all the flavors of the soup so well.

Serves
4 to 6

Cooking Time
5 + 15 Minutes

Release Method
Combo

2 cups dried white cannellini beans

4 ounces pancetta (or bacon if you can't find pancetta)

1 onion, finely diced

3 cloves garlic, minced

1 teaspoon dried thyme

1 teaspoon dried basil

½ teaspoon dried rosemary

2 tablespoons tomato paste

3 cups chicken stock

1 (28 ounce) can whole or diced tomatoes

4 ciabatta rolls, or 1 ciabatta baguette

olive oil

5 ounces fresh baby spinach, cleaned

1 teaspoon salt

freshly ground black pepper

block of Parmesan cheese

1. Place the beans in the pressure cooker and add water to cover the beans by one inch. Pressure cook on HIGH for 5 minutes. Let the pressure drop NATURALLY and carefully remove the lid. Drain the beans and set aside.

2. Pre-heat the pressure cooker using the BROWN setting.

3. Add the pancetta (or bacon) and cook until some of the fat has been rendered out. Add the onion, garlic, thyme, basil and rosemary and cook until the onion starts to soften. Add the tomato paste and stir to blend well. Add the chicken stock, tomatoes, and return the beans to the pressure cooker. Lock the lid in place.

4. Pressure cook on HIGH for 15 minutes. While the soup is cooking, pre-heat the broiler and slice the ciabatta in half horizontally (if using a ciabatta baguette, slice into 3-inch pieces and then slice in half horizontally). Brush the cut surfaces of the ciabatta with olive oil and toast the bread under the broiler until nicely browned.

5. Reduce the pressure with the QUICK-RELEASE method and carefully remove the lid.

6. Stir the spinach into the soup and season to taste with salt and pepper. Place one toasted piece of ciabatta in each bowl. Ladle the soup over the bread and garnish by shaving Parmesan cheese on top with a vegetable peeler.

Manhattan Clam Chowder

Using canned baby clams makes this an easy soup to put together. It also means you can get more clams per spoonful than if you used clams in the shell.

Serves
4 to 6

Cooking Time
8 Minutes

Release Method
Quick-release

4 strips of bacon, chopped

1 onion, finely chopped

1 carrot, finely chopped

2 ribs of celery, finely chopped

2 cloves garlic, minced

1 green bell pepper, chopped

1 teaspoon dried thyme

2 russet potatoes, peeled and chopped

1½ cups clam juice

1½ cups chicken stock

1 (14 ounce) can diced tomatoes

1 (14 ounce) can crushed tomatoes

2 (10 ounce) cans of baby clams, drained and rinsed

salt

freshly ground black pepper

¼ cup chopped fresh parsley

1. Pre-heat the pressure cooker using the BROWN setting.

2. Cook the bacon in the cooker until most of the fat has been rendered out. Add the onion, carrot, celery, garlic, bell pepper and thyme and cook until the onion is tender.

3. Add the potatoes, clam juice, chicken stock, tomatoes and clams to the cooker. Season with salt and pepper and lock the lid in place.

4. Pressure cook on HIGH for 8 minutes.

5. Reduce the pressure with the QUICK-RELEASE method and carefully remove the lid.

6. Stir the soup well, smashing some of the potato to thicken the soup. Season to taste again with salt and pepper and stir in the parsley.

Clam juice can be found in the grocery store in the same aisle as the tinned seafood.

Split Pea and Ham Soup

My mother often used to make split pea soup for Sunday lunches when I was a kid. Split pea soup with a hunk of crusty French bread is perfect comfort food for me now.

Serves
4 to 6

Cooking Time
10 Minutes

Release Method
Natural-release

1 tablespoon oil

1 onion, chopped

2 stalks of celery, chopped

2 cloves garlic, minced

1 teaspoon dried thyme

2 cups dried green split peas (1 pound)

1 ham bone or smoked pork hock, rinsed

6 cups water

salt and freshly ground black pepper

1 cup diced cooked ham (about 5 ounces)

1. Pre-heat the pressure cooker using the BROWN setting.

2. Add the oil to the pressure cooker and then cook the onion, celery, garlic and thyme until the vegetables just begin to soften. Add the split peas, ham bone and the water, and lock the lid in place.

3. Pressure cook on HIGH for 10 minutes.

4. Let the pressure drop NATURALLY and carefully remove the lid.

5. Remove the ham bone from the pot and let it cool enough to pull any meat from the bone. Set the meat aside.

6. Meanwhile, using a blender or an immersion blender, purée the soup. Season to taste with salt and pepper and thin the soup with a little water if necessary. Add the cooked ham and return any meat pulled from the ham bone. Serve with some crusty bread and a green salad.

Look for pork hocks in the frozen meat section of your grocery store. The pork hock adds a great flavor to the soup, but if you can't find one, don't fret – it will still be tasty with the ham added at the end.

Quinoa Chili
with Kidney Beans and Corn

This is a delicious vegetarian chili! Quinoa is a complete protein – supplying all nine essential amino acids – and turns this into a chili that fills you up and keeps you full.

Serves
6 to 8

Cooking Time
4 + 10 Minutes

Release Method
Combo

1 cup dried kidney beans

2 tablespoons olive oil

1 onion, diced

3 cloves garlic, minced

2 red bell peppers, chopped

1 green bell pepper, chopped

1 Jalapeño pepper, sliced (leave the seeds in if you like a spicier chili)

1 teaspoon dried oregano

2 tablespoons chili powder

1 tablespoon salt

1 cup quinoa, rinsed

2 tablespoons tomato paste

1 (28-ounce) can tomatoes, chopped

2¼ cups vegetable stock

2 cups corn kernels (fresh, or frozen and thawed)

½ cup chopped fresh cilantro or parsley

sour cream and diced avocado
(for garnish)

1. Place the beans in the pressure cooker and add enough water to cover the beans by one inch. Pressure cook on HIGH for 4 minutes. Let the pressure drop NATURALLY and carefully remove the lid. Drain the beans and set aside.

2. Pre-heat the pressure cooker using the BROWN setting.

3. Add the oil and sauté the onion and garlic until the onion starts to become tender – about 5 minutes. Add the peppers and spices and continue to cook for a few minutes. Stir in the quinoa, tomato paste, tomatoes and stock. Return the beans to the cooker, stir and lock the lid in place.

4. Pressure cook on HIGH for 10 minutes.

5. Release the pressure using the QUICK-RELEASE method and carefully remove the lid. Stir in the corn kernels and let them heat through. Season to taste with salt and stir in the fresh cilantro or parsley. Serve with sour cream and diced avocado.

The quinoa will continue to absorb liquid as it sits, so if you're saving leftovers of this chili, be sure to thin the soup with some water when you re-heat it.

Black Bean and Mushroom Chili

Button mushrooms, Crimini (brown) mushrooms and Portobello mushrooms are actually the same variety of mushroom, but at different stages of maturity. A white button mushroom is an immature version of a brown Crimini mushroom, which in turn is an immature version of a Portobello mushroom. I prefer the deeper, earthier flavor of brown mushrooms to white mushrooms, so that's what is called for here.

Serves
4 to 6

Cooking Time
3 + 8 Minutes

Release Method
Combo

1 cup dried black beans

1 tablespoon olive oil

1 onion, chopped

2 ribs celery, chopped

2 large cloves garlic, minced

1 red bell pepper, chopped

12 ounces Portobello, Crimini or brown mushrooms, quartered or cut into chunks

1 teaspoon dried ground cumin

1 teaspoon dried oregano

1 tablespoon chili powder

2 teaspoons salt

1 to 2 tablespoons chopped Chipotle peppers in adobo

1 (28 ounce) can tomatoes, chopped

1 cup vegetable stock

¼ cup fresh cilantro or parsley

sour cream, lime wedges, grated Cheddar cheese (for garnish)

1. Place the beans in the pressure cooker and add enough water to cover the beans by one inch. Pressure cook on HIGH for 3 minutes. Let the pressure drop NATURALLY and carefully remove the lid. Drain the beans and set aside.

2. Pre-heat the pressure cooker using the BROWN setting.

3. Add the olive oil and sauté the onion, celery, and garlic until the onion starts to become tender – about 5 minutes. Add the red pepper, mushrooms, spices and chipotle peppers and continue to cook for a few minutes. Add the tomatoes and vegetable stock, and return the beans to the pressure cooker. Lock the lid in place.

4. Pressure cook on HIGH for 8 minutes.

5. Let the pressure drop NATURALLY for 15 minutes. Then, release any residual pressure using the QUICK-RELEASE method and carefully remove the lid. Stir in the fresh cilantro or parsley. Serve with sour cream, lime wedges and Cheddar cheese.

If you decide to use Portobello mushrooms for this recipe, use a table spoon to scrape out the dark brown gills on the underside of the mushroom. While there's nothing wrong with eating the gills of the mushroom, they tend to make the finished dish very black in color – although that's not really an issue with this recipe either!

Chipotle Chickpea Chicken Chili

Not only is this a fun recipe name to say, it's a delcious meal too! You can use any combination of chicken pieces that you have on hand – breasts or legs. You can even use leftover chicken if you so chooose.

Serves
4 to 6

Cooking Time
5 + 20 Minutes

Release Method
Combo

1 cup dried chickpeas

1 tablespoon vegetable oil

1 yellow onion, chopped

2 ribs celery, chopped

1 large carrot, chopped

2 bell peppers (any combination of red, green, yellow or orange), chopped

2 large cloves garlic, minced

2 Chipotle chilies in adobo sauce, chopped

1 teaspoon dried ground cumin

½ teaspoon paprika (smoked paprika would be nice here)

1 tablespoon chili powder

2 teaspoons salt

1½ pounds chicken (breast, thigh or a combination of the two), cut into bite-sized pieces

1 (28 ounce) can whole tomatoes

1 cup chicken stock

2 tablespoons cornmeal

¼ cup fresh cilantro, chopped (or parsley)

1. Place the chickpeas in the pressure cooker and add water to cover the chickpeas by one inch. Pressure cook on HIGH for 5 minutes. Let the pressure drop NATURALLY and carefully remove the lid. Drain the chickpeas and set aside.

2. Pre-heat the pressure cooker using the BROWN setting.

3. Add the oil and sauté the onion, celery, carrot, peppers and garlic in the pressure cooker together for a few minutes. Add the chipotle chilies, dried cumin, paprika, chili powder and salt and stir well to coat all the vegetables in the spices. Stir in the chicken, return the chickpeas and add the tomatoes and chicken stock to the cooker. Lock the lid in place.

4. Pressure cook on HIGH for 20 minutes.

5. Reduce the pressure with the QUICK-RELEASE method and carefully remove the lid.

6. In a small bowl, mix the cornmeal with about ¼ cup of the liquid from the chili. Return this mixture into the chili while it is still hot and bubbling. Season again with salt to taste and stir in the fresh cilantro.

Chickpeas cooked from scratch tend to have more substance and are firmer than canned chickpeas. That's how I like them best. If you prefer canned chickpeas, however, just skip step 1 and add them in at the end of cooking when you add the cornmeal.

Chili con Carne

This chili includes beef and chorizo sausage – a Spanish sausage with a smoky flavor imparted by smoked red peppers. I like to use fresh chorizo in this recipe. If you can't find fresh chorizo, substitute your favorite hot Italian sausage instead.

Serves
4 to 6

Cooking Time
5 + 15 Minutes

Release Method
Combo

1 cup red kidney beans

2 tablespoons vegetable oil, divided

1 pound ground beef

8 ounces raw chorizo sausage, casing removed and crumbled

1 onion, finely chopped

2 ribs of celery, finely chopped

2 cloves garlic, minced

1 Jalapeño pepper, sliced

1 tablespoon chili powder

1 teaspoon dried oregano

½ teaspoon ground dried cumin

1 tablespoon tomato paste

1 (12 ounce) bottle of lager beer

1 (28 ounce) can whole tomatoes, drained and crushed by hand

1 cup beef stock

2 teaspoons salt

freshly ground black pepper

¼ cup chopped fresh cilantro (optional)

1. Place the beans in the pressure cooker and add enough water to cover the beans by one inch. Pressure cook on HIGH for 5 minutes. Let the pressure drop NATURALLY and carefully remove the lid. Drain the beans and set aside.

2. Pre-heat the pressure cooker using the BROWN setting.

3. Add one tablespoon of the oil and brown the beef and chorizo in batches, setting the meat aside when brown. Drain off the fat and add the remaining tablespoon of oil. Add the onion, celery, garlic, Jalapeño pepper and spices, and cook for another few minutes. Add the tomato paste, stir well and continue to cook for another minute. Add the beer, tomatoes, beef stock and return the beans and the browned meat to the cooker. Season with salt and pepper and lock the lid in place.

4. Pressure cook on HIGH for 15 minutes.

5. Release the pressure using the QUICK-RELEASE method and carefully remove the lid.

6. Season to taste again with salt and pepper. Serve with any of several garnishes: sour cream, fresh cilantro, shredded cheese, tomato salsa.

Chile Verde

Chili Verde is usually made with roasted tomatillos. Here we add a jar of tomatillo salsa, which includes other ingredients and spices that add flavor to the chili. The salsa has a huge role in this dish with respect to flavor and spiciness, so pick a salsa that suits your tastes.

Serves
6

Cooking Time
15 Minutes

Release Method
Natural

1 to 2 tablespoons vegetable oil

3 pounds pork butt or shoulder, trimmed of fat and cut into bite-sized pieces

salt, to taste

1 onion, rough chopped

2 Poblano peppers, diced

1 teaspoon dried oregano

½ teaspoon ground dried cumin

24 ounces jarred tomatillo salsa

1 cup chicken stock

¼ cup chopped fresh cilantro (or parsley)

1 cup sour cream

1. Pre-heat the pressure cooker on the BROWN setting.

2. Add one tablespoon of the oil and brown the pork pieces in batches, seasoning with salt and adding more oil as needed. Set the browned pork aside. Add the onion, Poblano pepper and spices and cook for another 5 minutes. Add the salsa and the chicken stock, return the pork to the cooker, stir well and lock the lid in place.

3. Pressure cook on HIGH for 15 minutes.

4. Let the pressure drop NATURALLY and carefully remove the lid. Season to taste again with salt and stir in the cilantro. Serve over rice and beans, or alone with a dollop of sour cream on top.

Poblano peppers are a mild flavored, dark green pepper. If you can't find Poblanos in your grocery store, use green bell peppers.

Pasta

Creamy Tomato Macaroni

Chili Macaroni

Chicken Alfredo Rotini

Cavatappi con Vongole

Quick and Easy Mac 'n' Cheese

Vegetarian Spinach and Squash Lasagna

Creamy Cheese Tortellini with Ham and Peas

Rigatoni, Italian Sausage, Sun-Dried Tomatoes, Artichokes

Cheesy Macaroni and Sweet Italian Sausage

Roaster Red Pepper Rigatoni with Feta Cheese

Creamy Tomato Macaroni

Creamy Tomato Macaroni (or tomato macaroni soup) is comfort food in Quebec to a certain generation. It was what you found at snackbars or roadside diners across the province. Simple and delicious, always buttery or creamy, it's bound to please everyone in the family.

Serves
4

Cooking Time
5 Minutes

Release Method
Quick-release

3 tablespoons butter

½ onion, finely diced (about ½ cup)

½ cup finely diced celery

1 garlic clove, smashed

1 teaspoon dried basil

½ teaspoon salt

1 tablespoon tomato paste

1 (28-ounce) can tomatoes, chopped

1 cup chicken stock

2 cups elbow macaroni (about 8 ounces)

½ cup heavy cream

salt and freshly ground black pepper

grated Parmesan cheese

1. Pre-heat the pressure cooker using the BROWN setting.

2. Add the butter, onion, celery, garlic, basil and salt and sauté until the vegetables start to soften – about 5 minutes. Add the tomato paste and continue to cook for another 2 to 3 minutes.

3. Add tomatoes, chicken stock and dried pasta. Stir and lock the lid in place.

4. Pressure cook on HIGH for 5 minutes.

5. Release the pressure using the QUICK-RELEASE method and carefully remove the lid. Stir in the heavy cream and season to taste with salt and pepper. Let the pasta sit in the cooker for about 5 minutes or until it is cool enough to eat. Serve with the grated Parmesan cheese sprinkled on top.

Lighten Up

Try using half-and-half or milk in this recipe instead of the heavy cream for a lighter meal.

Chili Macaroni

Everyone loves a chili mac – the classic combination of chili and macaroni and cheese. Making it in the pressure cooker means that you can love it sooner – in just 5 minutes!

Serves
4 to 6

Cooking Time
5 Minutes

Release Method
Quick-release

1 tablespoon vegetable oil

1 pound lean ground beef

1 onion, finely chopped

2 cloves garlic, minced

1 red bell pepper, chopped

1 yellow bell pepper, chopped

1 Jalapeño pepper, sliced with or without the seeds (optional)

3 tablespoons chili powder

¼ teaspoon cayenne pepper

1 teaspoon salt

1 (28-ounce) can tomatoes, chopped

1 cup beef stock

1 (15-ounce) can kidney beans, drained and rinsed

2 cups elbow macaroni (about 8 ounces)

salt and freshly ground black pepper

2 cups grated Pepperjack or Cheddar cheese

sour cream for garnish (optional)

1. Pre-heat the pressure cooker using the BROWN setting.

2. Add the oil and brown the beef, breaking it up as you do. Add the onion, garlic, bell peppers, Jalapeño pepper, chili powder, cayenne pepper and salt and cook for just a couple minutes more. Stir in the tomatoes, beef stock, beans and macaroni, and lock the lid in place.

3. Pressure cook on HIGH for 5 minutes.

4. Release the pressure using the QUICK-RELEASE method and carefully remove the lid. Give the ingredients a good stir and season to taste with more salt and freshly ground black pepper. Stir in the grated cheese and serve with a dollop of sour cream if you like.

You can use dried beans for this recipe instead of the canned kidney beans. Cook ½ cup of dried kidney beans, covered with water, at HIGH pressure in the cooker for 6 minutes. Let the pressure release NATURALLY. Then drain and proceed with the recipe as written.

Chicken Alfredo Rotini

If you like pasta and you like cheese, any Alfredo recipe is pretty tough to turn down! This one is no exception. Try adding other flavors to the Alfredo at the end if you like – sun-dried tomatoes, peas, cooked broccoli florets.

Serves
2 to 4

Cooking Time
6 Minutes

Release Method
Quick-release

¼ cup butter

½ cup onion, diced

1 clove garlic, minced

2 large boneless skinless chicken breasts, cut in large cubes

salt and freshly ground black pepper

2 cups chicken stock

1½ cups heavy cream

8 ounces rotini pasta (about 2½ to 3 cups)

½ teaspoon salt

1¼ cups grated Parmigiano-Reggiano cheese, divided

2 tablespoons chopped fresh parsley (optional)

1. Pre-heat the pressure cooker using the BROWN setting.

2. Add the butter to the cooker and sauté the onions and garlic until they just start to brown. Add the chicken, season with salt and freshly ground black pepper and cook for a minute or two. Then, add the chicken stock, heavy cream, rotini pasta and salt. Stir to combine ingredients and lock the lid in place.

3. Pressure cook on HIGH for 6 minutes.

4. Release pressure using the QUICK-RELEASE method and carefully remove the lid. Immediately stir in the Parmigiano-Reggiano cheese and the parsley, if using. Season to taste with salt and lots of freshly ground black pepper. Let the pasta sit for 5 minutes. It will cool to an edible temperature and continue to absorb more liquid. Serve with more cheese at the table.

Not all Parmesan cheeses are created equal! When the flavor of the Parmesan cheese is critical to the success of the dish (as it is in this recipe), make sure you use the very best Parmesan cheese that you can. One that has "Parmigiano-Reggiano" printed on the rind and has been aged for at least a year is perfect.

Cavatappi con Vongole
(Pasta with Clams)

When I was a little girl, my mother used to make spaghetti con vongole and it was one of my favorite pastas. I liked the way it tasted and I LOVED just saying the name! Here's a version using fresh clams and curly cavatappi pasta.

Serves
2 to 4

Cooking Time
4 Minutes

Release Method
Quick-release

2 pounds (about 24) fresh littleneck or Manila clams

2 tablespoons olive oil

2 cloves garlic, sliced

⅛ to ¼ teaspoon crushed red pepper flakes

1 cup white wine

1 cup chicken stock

8 ounces cavatappi pasta (about 2 heaping cups)

2 cups halved cherry tomatoes

½ cup coarse or panko breadcrumbs

4 tablespoons butter, divided

½ lemon, zest and juice

salt and freshly ground black pepper

½ cup chopped fresh parsley

extra virgin olive oil

1. Before you start cooking or prepping, soak the clams in tap water (room temperature). Let them soak while you prepare the rest of the recipe, or for at least 30 minutes. They will spit out sand. Then, pick the clams out of the water and give the shells a scrub under running water to remove any barnacles or dirt. Discard any clams that are open or have cracked shells.

2. Add the olive oil, garlic and crushed red pepper flakes to the pressure cooker and then pre-heat the pressure cooker using the BROWN setting. Just before the garlic starts to turn brown on the edges, add the wine and bring to a simmer. Then, add the stock, pasta and tomatoes. Place the clams on top and lock the lid in place.

3. Pressure cook on HIGH for 4 minutes.

4. While the pasta is cooking, toast the breadcrumbs in 2 table-spoons of butter using a small skillet over medium heat. Set aside when nicely browned and crunchy.

5. Release the pressure using the QUICK-RELEASE method and carefully remove the lid. Remove the clams to a serving bowl with a big slotted spoon, discarding any clams that did not fully open. Add the remaining butter and lemon juice to the pot and season the broth to taste with salt and freshly ground black pepper. Toss the clams and pasta together and pour the broth over the top. Sprinkle the chopped parsley, lemon zest and toasted breadcrumbs on top, drizzle with olive oil and don't forget to put a bowl on the table for everyone's clamshells!

Yes, traditionally pasta con vongole is made with spaghetti. However, you can't cook long pasta like spaghetti in a pressure cooker, so this recipe uses a small-shaped pasta. If you can't find cavatappi in your grocery store, choose another shape of pasta with an 8-minute cooking time.

Quick and Easy Mac 'n' Cheese

This is the easiest Mac 'n' Cheese ever!

Serves
4 to 6

Cooking Time
6 Minutes

Release Method
Quick-release

1 tablespoon olive oil

1 pound macaroni (about 4 cups)

2½ cups water

½ cup heavy cream

1½ cups grated Cheddar cheese

½ cup grated Parmesan cheese

2 ounces cream cheese

salt and freshly ground pepper

¼ cup fresh parsley, chopped

1. Pre-heat the pressure cooker using the BROWN setting.

2. Add the oil and stir in the dry macaroni to coat. Pour in the water and lock the lid in place.

3. Pressure cook on HIGH for 6 minutes.

4. Reduce the pressure with QUICK-RELEASE method and carefully remove the lid.

5. Immediately add all remaining ingredients and stir well. Season to taste with salt and pepper and garnish with freshly chopped parsley.

 *Dress It Up*

It's easy to mix things up with this recipe for Mac 'n' Cheese by just adding cooked ingredients at the end. Try stirring in cooked bacon, cherry tomatoes, caramelized onion or any combination of ingredients.

Vegetarian Spinach and Squash Lasagna

It is tempting to make a lasagna directly in a pressure cooker, but it can be tricky as it sometimes burns a little on the bottom. This lasagna is built in a dish that you can take right to the table for serving family style.

Serves
6

Cooking Time
35 Minutes

Release Method
Quick-release

1 pound ricotta cheese

¼ cup grated Parmesan cheese

2½ cups grated mozzarella cheese, divided

1 egg, lightly beaten

½ teaspoon salt

freshly ground black pepper

10 ounces frozen chopped spinach, thawed and drained

12 lasagna noodles

1 (24-ounce) jar marinara sauce

½ zucchini, thinly sliced

½ yellow squash, thinly sliced

1 carrot shredded

1 red pepper, chopped

½ teaspoon dried oregano

1. In large bowl, mix the ricotta cheese, the Parmesan cheese, and one cup of the mozzarella cheese together with the egg, salt and freshly ground black pepper. Squeeze as much of the water out of the chopped spinach as you can and mix it into the cheese mixture.

2. Butter or oil the inside of a round baking dish that will fit in your pressure cooker. Build the lasagna as follows:

- Marinara sauce to cover the bottom of the dish
- Three lasagna noodles, broken as needed to cover the bottom of the dish
- Half the ricotta cheese mixture
- Half the zucchini and yellow squash
- Half the shredded carrots and red pepper
- …(repeat the above five layers, and then continue with)…
- Another layer of marinara sauce
- Three lasagna noodles, broken as needed to cover the bottom of the dish
- Another layer of marinara sauce
- The remaining grated Mozzarella cheese
- Sprinkle the dried oregano on top

3. Spray a piece of aluminum foil with cooking spray and loosely cover the lasagna.

4. Place a rack in the bottom of the pressure cooker and add 2 cups of water. Lower the casserole into the cooker using a sling made of aluminum foil (fold a piece of aluminum foil into a strip about 2 inches wide by 24 inches long). Fold the ends of the aluminum foil into the cooker and lock the lid into place.

5. Pressure cook on HIGH for 35 minutes.

6. Release the pressure using the QUICK-RELEASE method and carefully remove the lid. Remove lasagna from cooker, using the aluminum foil sling and let the lasagna sit for at least 15 minutes before serving.

Creamy Cheese Tortellini with Ham and Peas

Pasta with cream, ham and peas is so delicious, but when the pasta is cheese tortellini it's even more decadent and creamy.

Serves
4

Cooking Time
4 Minutes

Release Method
Quick-release

3 tablespoons butter

½ onion, finely chopped

1 clove garlic, minced

½ cup heavy cream

1 cup chicken stock

12 ounces frozen cheese tortellini

1 cup diced cooked ham (about 5 ounces)

½ teaspoon salt

freshly ground black pepper

1 tablespoon butter, softened

1 tablespoon flour

¼ cup grated Parmesan cheese

½ cup frozen peas

1. Preheat the pressure cooker using the BROWN setting.

2. Add the three tablespoons of butter to the cooker and cook the onions and garlic for a few minutes, until the onion starts to soften. Add the heavy cream, stock, frozen tortellini, ham, salt and freshly ground black pepper, and stir well.

3. Pressure cook on HIGH for 4 minutes.

4. While the tortellini is cooking, combine the remaining tablespoon of softened butter with the flour and mix it into a paste.

5. Release pressure using the QUICK RELEASE method and carefully remove the lid. Remove and discard half a cup of the hot liquid from pressure cooker. Return the cooker to the BROWN setting and stir in the butter-flour paste, the Parmesan cheese and the peas. Once the sauce has thickened and the cheese has melted, turn the cooker off, season with salt and freshly ground black pepper and serve.

Rigatoni with Italian Sausage, Sun-Dried Tomatoes and Artichokes

This might be one of my all-time favorite pasta sauces. Here, the pasta cooks right in with the sauce, soaking up all the delicious flavors.

Serves
4

Cooking Time
7 Minutes

Release Method
Quick-release

1 pound hot Italian sausage, casings removed and crumbled

1 red bell pepper, cut into large chunks

1 yellow bell pepper, cut into large chunks

1 clove garlic, minced

pinch crushed red pepper flakes

¼ cup red wine

1¾ cups chicken stock

1 (28 ounce) can crushed tomatoes

½ cup sliced sun-dried tomatoes

1 (6- ounce) jar artichokes (marinated or water packed), drained

8 ounces dried rigatoni pasta (about 3 cups)

salt and freshly ground black pepper

grated Parmesan cheese (optional)

1. Pre-heat the pressure cooker using the BROWN setting.

2. Add the crumbled sausage and cook until browned. Remove the sausage with a slotted spoon and set aside. Add the peppers, garlic and red pepper flakes to the cooker and cook for a few minutes. Add the wine and bring to a simmer. Add the chicken stock, crushed tomatoes, sun-dried tomatoes and artichokes, and return the sausage to the pan. Stir in the rigatoni, pushing it under the liquid and lock the lid in place.

3. Pressure cook on HIGH for 7 minutes.

4. Reduce the pressure using the QUICK-RELEASE method and carefully remove the lid.

5. Season to taste with salt and freshly ground black pepper. Serve with Parmesan cheese.

Cheesy Macaroni and Sweet Italian Sausage

The ketchup in this recipe gives a sweet note to the pasta that will keep you coming back for more. It's a terrific one dish meal that the whole family will enjoy.

Serves
6

Cooking Time
6 Minutes

Release Method
Quick-release

1 tablespoon vegetable oil

1 pound sweet Italian sausage, casings removed and broken into chunks

1 onion, finely chopped

1 yellow bell pepper, chopped

1 red bell pepper, chopped

1½ teaspoons dried oregano

1½ teaspoons dried basil

1 teaspoon paprika

1 teaspoon salt

freshly ground black pepper

1 (28 ounce) can diced tomatoes

1 cup beef stock

¼ cup ketchup

12 ounces dried elbow macaroni (about 3 cups)

grated Parmesan cheese OR
1½ cups grated Cheddar cheese

1. Pre-heat the pressure cooker using the BROWN setting.

2. Add the oil to the cooker and brown the sausage. Add the onion, peppers, herbs and spices, salt and pepper and continue to cook for a few minutes, stirring well. Add the tomatoes, stock, ketchup and elbow macaroni and lock the lid in place.

3. Pressure cook on HIGH for 6 minutes.

4. Reduce the pressure with the QUICK-RELEASE method and carefully remove the lid.

5. Give the ingredients a good stir, season to taste with salt and pepper, and serve with grated Parmesan cheese or for a cheesier dish, stir in the grated Cheddar cheese. Let everything rest for a few minutes before serving.

Roasted Red Pepper Rigatoni with Feta Cheese

Here's another super easy pasta recipe that can be made in less than ten minutes using dried pasta. You can definitely substitute an onion for the leek here, but the leek does add a nice gentle note to the dish, along with a touch of color.

Serves
4 to 6

Cooking Time
7 Minutes

Release Method
Quick-release

1 tablespoon olive oil

1 leek, chopped

1 clove garlic, sliced

1 teaspoon dried basil

1 teaspoon salt

1 (15.5-ounce) jar roasted red peppers (about 5 whole roasted peppers), sliced

3 fresh tomatoes, chopped

2 cups chicken stock

8 ounces rigatoni pasta (about 3 cups)

freshly ground black pepper

½ cup cream

1 cup crumbled feta cheese

¼ cup chopped fresh parsley or basil

1. Pre-heat the pressure cooker using the BROWN setting.

2. Add the olive oil and sauté the leek, garlic, basil, and salt for 2 to 3 minutes. Add the roasted red peppers, tomatoes, stock and dried pasta. Season with freshly ground black pepper and stir everything together. Lock the lid in place.

3. Pressure cook on HIGH for 7 minutes.

4. Release the pressure using the QUICK-RELEASE method and carefully remove the lid. Stir in the cream and feta cheese and let the pasta cool to an edible temperature for a couple of minutes. Garnish with fresh parsley or basil and enjoy!

Did You Know...?

Leeks are the elegant, mild-flavored member of the onion family. They can be dirty, however, getting soil caught between their leaves as they push up out of the ground. Make sure you clean them well by cutting off the dark green top of the leek where it naturally wants to break if you bend the leek from end to end. Then, slice the leek in half lengthwise and soak it in cold water for 10 minutes or so, separating the leaves with your hands to remove any embedded dirt. Dry the leeks with a paper towel gently before using.

Poultry

Salsa Chicken Thighs with Rice
Thai Peanut Chicken and Shrimp
Chili-Rubbed Chicken Legs with Roasted Red Pepper Quinoa
BBQ Wings
Chicken Paprikash
Chicken with Prunes, Capers and Olives
Greek Chicken and Potatoes
BBQ Pulled Chicken
Curried Chicken with Cauliflower, Peas and Basil
Jerk Spiced Chicken Legs with Rice
Chicken and Lemon-Chive Dumplings
Whole Chicken with Marinara and Vegetables
Chicken Breasts Florentine with Mushrooms
Chicken Tikka Masala

Salsa Chicken Thighs with Rice

The flavor and spiciness of this super easy dish depends entirely on the salsa that you use. So buy a salsa that you like and make sure it is the right level of spiciness for you. If you'd like it even spicier, add a sliced Jalapeño pepper to the rice with the bell peppers.

Serves
2 to 4

Cooking Time
5 Minutes

Release Method
Quick-release

4 large (or 8 small) skinless chicken thighs

1 teaspoon salt

½ teaspoon chili powder

1 tablespoon olive oil

½ red onion, finely chopped (about ½ cup)

1 red bell pepper, finely diced

1 green bell pepper, finely diced

1 cup basmati rice (regular long-grain white rice can be substituted)

1 cup chicken stock

¾ cup jarred salsa

½ cup grated Monterey Jack cheese (about 3 ounces)

¼ cup chopped fresh cilantro

1. Pre-heat the pressure cooker using the BROWN setting.

2. Season the chicken thighs with the salt and chili powder. Add the oil to the cooker and sear the thighs on both sides until well browned. Remove the chicken from the cooker and set aside. Add the onion and peppers and sauté until the onion starts to become tender – about 5 minutes. Add the rice and stir well to coat everything with the oil. Season the rice with salt, pour in the chicken stock and return the chicken thighs to the cooker, resting them on top of the rice. Top each chicken thigh with the salsa and lock the lid in place.

3. Pressure cook on HIGH for 5 minutes.

4. Release the pressure using the QUICK-RELEASE method and carefully remove the lid. Sprinkle the cheese on top of the thighs and return the lid to the cooker for another 5 minutes while the chicken rests and cools to an edible temperature. Transfer the chicken thighs and rice to a serving platter and sprinkle the cilantro on top before serving.

Cooking chicken with the bone in produces a more flavorful result. In the pressure cooker, skin doesn't have a chance to get crispy, so I tend to use chicken that is skinless, but still on the bone.

Thai Peanut Chicken and Shrimp

It may seem silly to have a cooking time of just one minute, but when you include the time it takes for the cooker to come to pressure, it's just the right amount of time to cook both the shrimp and chicken strips perfectly.

Serves
4

Cooking Time
1 Minute

Release Method
Quick-release

1 tablespoon canola or vegetable oil

½ onion, finely diced

1 clove garlic, minced

1 tablespoon grated fresh ginger

2 tablespoons soy sauce

1 tablespoon chili garlic sauce

¼ cup natural creamy peanut butter

1 tablespoon brown sugar

1 tablespoon cider vinegar

1 cup chicken stock

1½ pound boneless skinless chicken breasts, cut into thin strips

12 large shrimp

2 carrots, peeled and julienned (cut into matchsticks)

2 tablespoons cornstarch

fresh cilantro or basil leaves

scallions, sliced on the bias

hot red chili pepper, thinly sliced into rings or strips

roasted, salted peanuts

lime wedges

1. Pre-heat the pressure cooker using the BROWN setting.

2. Add the oil to the cooker and sauté the onion, garlic and ginger for a couple of minutes. Add the soy sauce, chili garlic sauce, peanut butter, brown sugar, cider vinegar and stock. Stir well. Add the chicken, shrimp and carrots, and lock the lid in place.

3. Pressure cook on HIGH for just 1 minute.

4. While the chicken and shrimp are cooking, combine the cornstarch with 2 tablespoons of water in a small bowl.

5. Release the pressure using the QUICK-RELEASE method and carefully remove the lid. Turn the cooker onto the BROWN setting again and stir in the cornstarch mixture. Bring the sauce to a simmer so that it thickens slightly and then immediately turn the cooker off. Serve over noodles or rice in bowls with the cilantro, scallions, red chili pepper and peanuts on top, and a lime wedge on the side.

Chili-Rubbed Chicken Legs with Roasted Red Pepper Quinoa

You can make many different dishes with this one recipe, just by changing the spice rub and adding different ingredients to the quinoa. Try an herb rub on the chicken and sun dried tomatoes in the quinoa for a Provençal twist with some fresh basil sprinkled on top.

Serves
4

Cooking Time
8 Minutes

Release Method
Quick-release

2 teaspoons chili powder

1 teaspoon smoked paprika

2 teaspoons salt

4 chicken legs, drumsticks and thighs separated

2 tablespoons vegetable oil

1 onion, finely chopped

1 cup roasted red pepper strips, chopped

½ teaspoon dried thyme

1 cup quinoa, rinsed

1¾ cups chicken stock

1 teaspoon salt

freshly ground black pepper

¼ cup chopped fresh parsley

1. Combine the chili powder, paprika and salt in a zipper lock plastic bag. Add the chicken thighs and drumsticks and shake around until evenly coated. If you have time to leave the chicken with the rub for up to 30 minutes, do so. Otherwise, proceed with the recipe.

2. Pre-heat the pressure cooker using the BROWN setting.

3. Add one tablespoon of the oil to the cooker and sear the chicken until well browned on all sides. You'll need to do this in batches. Remove the browned chicken to a side plate and reserve.

4. Add the remaining oil to the cooker and cook the onion for a few minutes, until it starts to soften. Add the roasted red pepper strips and thyme and stir. Add the quinoa and stir to coat with the oil. Add the chicken stock and salt and then return the chicken legs to the cooker, placing them on top of the quinoa. Lock the lid in place.

5. Pressure cook on HIGH for 8 minutes.

6. Release the pressure using the QUICK-RELEASE method and carefully remove the lid. Remove the chicken to a side plate and fluff the quinoa with a fork. Serve the chicken and quinoa together and sprinkle with chopped parsley.

BBQ Chicken Wings

While you don't have to pop these under the broiler before serving, I really like them better when you do. It enhances the flavor and adds a few brown crunchy bits.

Serves
4

Cooking Time
6 Minutes

Release Method
Quick-release

1 to 2 tablespoons vegetable oil

1 onion, finely chopped

3 cloves garlic, minced

½ teaspoon paprika

½ teaspoon chili powder

½ teaspoon dry mustard powder

¼ teaspoon ground cayenne pepper

1 cup ketchup

1 tablespoon tomato paste

2 tablespoons brown sugar

2 tablespoons apple cider vinegar

1 cup chicken stock

1 teaspoon salt

4 pounds chicken wings, wing tips trimmed off and discarded

salt and freshly ground black pepper

1. Pre-heat the pressure cooker using the BROWN setting.

2. Add the oil to the cooker and cook the onion and garlic for a minute or two. Add the dry spices and continue to cook for a few minutes. Add the ketchup, tomato paste, brown sugar, cider vinegar, chicken stock and salt, stirring well to combine and scraping the bottom of the cooker to stir in any brown bits. Pour the sauce over the chicken wings in a bowl and then transfer the wings and sauce back to the cooker. Lock the lid in place.

3. Pressure cook on HIGH for 6 minutes.

4. Release the pressure using the QUICK-RELEASE method and carefully remove the lid.

5. Transfer the wings to a baking sheet and return the pressure cooker to the BROWN setting to let the sauce simmer and thicken. When the sauce has reached a good sauce consistency, baste the wings with the sauce and broil each side for 3 to 5 minutes until nicely browned. Serve with a blue cheese dip and celery stalks.

 Did You Know...?

If you find your brown sugar has hardened in its container, add a slice of apple to the container for a few hours and the brown sugar will be soft again in a jiffy.

Chicken Paprikash

I first tasted Chicken Paprikash when I worked in a restaurant in Kingston, Ontario owned by two Czechoslovakian chefs. Though Paprikash is of Hungarian origin, my two Czech chefs made a lot of eastern European dishes and did it so well. We all loved Chicken Paprikash day! This version veers slightly from the traditional by including red pepper.

Serves
4

Cooking Time
6 Minutes

Release Method
Quick-release

1 tablespoon vegetable oil

4 boneless skinless chicken breasts, sliced into 1-inch strips

½ onion, finely chopped

1 red bell pepper, sliced

1 clove garlic, minced

2 tablespoons paprika

1 (28 ounce) can whole tomatoes

1 cup chicken stock

1 tablespoon butter, softened

2 tablespoons flour

1 cup sour cream

1 teaspoon salt

freshly ground black pepper

¼ cup chopped fresh parsley

1. Pre-heat the pressure cooker using the BROWN setting.

2. Add the oil and sear the chicken pieces until lightly brown. Remove and set aside.

3. Add the onion, bell pepper and garlic to the cooker and cook until tender. Stir in the paprika and cook for another minute. Add the tomatoes and chicken stock and stir well to scrape up any brown bits from the bottom of the cooker. Return the chicken to the pressure cooker and lock the lid in place.

4. Pressure cook on HIGH for 6 minutes.

5. Release the pressure using the QUICK-RELEASE method and carefully remove the lid.

6. In a small bowl, combine the flour with the softened butter until it forms a paste. Add ¼ cup of the hot liquid from the pressure cooker and whisk well. Return this mixture to the cooker while the sauce is still hot and bubbling. Stir in the sour cream, season with salt and freshly ground black pepper and garnish with fresh parsley.

While browning the chicken strips first does add flavor, you can skip this step if you're in a rush. Just add the chicken strips when you add the tomatoes and stock and stir well before locking the lid in place.

Hungarians take their paprika seriously, and Hungarian paprika is considered to be the finest in the world. Because most of the flavor in this dish comes from paprika, I highly recommend getting the best Hungarian paprika that you can find.

Chicken with Prunes, Capers and Olives

The Silver Palate Cookbook, by Julee Rosso and Sheila Lukins, is a classic among cookbooks. Their Chicken Marbella is one of my favorites, so here it is adapted for the pressure cooker.

Serves
4

Cooking Time
9 Minutes

Release Method
Quick-release

2 tablespoons olive oil

3 pounds chicken breasts or legs, bone in, but skin removed

salt and freshly ground black pepper

1 onion, sliced

3 cloves garlic, minced

1 cup pitted prunes

½ cup pitted green olives

½ cup capers, drained and rinsed

2 teaspoons dried oregano

2 bay leaves

¼ cup brown sugar

1 cup white wine

2 tablespoons red wine vinegar

½ cup chicken stock

¼ cup chopped fresh parsley

1. Pre-heat the pressure cooker using the BROWN setting.

2. Add the olive oil. Season the chicken with salt and pepper and sear in batches until well browned on all sides. Remove the browned chicken to a plate and set aside.

3. Add the onion and garlic to the cooker and cook until the onion starts to soften. Add the prunes, olives, capers, oregano, bay leaves and brown sugar and continue to cook for a minute. Pour in the white wine and red wine vinegar and bring to a simmer for a minute. Add the chicken stock, return the chicken to the cooker and lock the lid in place.

4. Pressure cook on HIGH for 9 minutes.

5. Release the pressure using the QUICK-RELEASE method and carefully remove the lid.

6. Season to taste with salt and pepper and serve with fresh parsley sprinkled on top.

Capers come either packed in salt or in a salty brine. Either way, don't forget to rinse them before you use them.

Greek Chicken and Potatoes

We don't generally put cinnamon in many savory dishes in American or Canadian cuisine, but it's a common occurrence in Greek foods. I think it adds a lot of interest to a dish, even when you add just a small amount as in the recipe below.

Serves
4

Cooking Time
8 Minutes

Release Method
Quick-release

1 tablespoon olive oil

4 boneless, skinless chicken breasts, each cut into two chunks

salt and freshly ground black pepper

1 onion, chopped

1 clove garlic, sliced

2 red bell peppers, julienned

1 teaspoon dried oregano

1 bay leaf

1 teaspoon salt

2 tablespoons tomato paste

¼ teaspoon ground cinnamon

½ cup white wine

1½ cups chicken stock

1 (14-ounce) can crushed tomatoes

2 russet potatoes, peeled and cut into 1-inch wide wedges

1 cup crumbled feta cheese

¼ cup chopped fresh parsley

1. Pre-heat the pressure cooker using the BROWN setting.

2. Add the olive oil to the cooker. Season the chicken with salt and pepper and brown for about 2 minutes per side. Remove the chicken and set aside.

3. Add the onion, garlic, red pepper and oregano to the cooker and cook for 3 to 4 minutes. Add the bay leaf, salt, tomato paste and cinnamon and cook for 2 more minutes. Add the white wine and bring to a simmer for a couple of minutes. Add the chicken stock, tomatoes and potatoes to the cooker and stir. Return the chicken to the pot and lock the lid in place.

4. Pressure cook on HIGH for 8 minutes.

5. Release the pressure using the QUICK-RELEASE method and carefully remove the lid. Let the chicken cool to an edible temperature and serve with feta cheese and parsley sprinkled on top.

 *Shortcut*

In a rush? You can skip the browning step in the recipe and just put the un-browned chicken into the cooker in step 4 instead. It may not be as attractive, but it will be covered with tomato sauce and you can always just turn the lights down low.

BBQ Pulled Chicken

You can use chicken breasts or thighs for this dish. I think it's nice to have a little of each. This is a nice lighter version of pulled pork with a tangy rather than thick and sweet sauce.

Serves
4 to 6

Cooking Time
10 Minutes

Release Method
Quick-release

6 strips bacon, chopped

3 boneless skinless chicken breasts, cut in half

4 boneless skinless chicken thighs

salt and freshly ground black pepper

1 onion, finely chopped

3 cloves garlic, minced

½ teaspoon smoked paprika

½ teaspoon chili powder

½ teaspoon dry mustard powder

¼ teaspoon ground cayenne pepper

1 cup ketchup

1 tablespoon tomato paste

2 tablespoons brown sugar

¼ cup apple cider vinegar

¼ cup chicken stock

1 teaspoon salt

1. Pre-heat the pressure cooker using the BROWN setting.

2. Add the bacon and cook until crispy. Remove the bacon with a slotted spoon and set aside. Season the chicken with salt and pepper and add to the cooker, searing in batches until well browned on all sides. Remove the browned chicken to a plate and set aside.

3. Add the onion and garlic to the pressure cooker and cook until tender. Add the dry spices and continue to cook for a few minutes. Add the remaining ingredients, stirring well to combine and scraping the bottom of the cooker to stir in any brown bits. Return the chicken to the cooker and lock the lid in place.

4. Pressure cook on HIGH for 10 minutes.

5. Release the pressure using the QUICK-RELEASE method and carefully remove the lid.

6. Remove the chicken to a side plate. Once cool, shred the chicken using two forks or by hand. Add sauce to the chicken until you achieve the desired consistency. Add the reserved cooked bacon to the chicken or save it for another use.

 Substitution

Smoked paprika is pretty easily found in the super-market these days and gives this pulled chicken a smoky note without having to put it on the BBQ. But, if you can't find smoked paprika, regular sweet paprika will do.

Curried Chicken with Cauliflower, Peas and Basil

Serves
4

Cooking Time
4 Minutes

Release Method
Quick-release

1 tablespoon vegetable oil

1 tablespoon butter

1 sweet onion, finely chopped

3 cloves garlic, minced

1 inch fresh gingerroot, grated

2 tablespoons curry powder

⅛ teaspoon ground cayenne pepper

2 tablespoons tomato paste

2 boneless skinless chicken breasts, cut into bite-sized pieces

1 Granny Smith apple, peeled and diced

½ cup golden raisins (or black raisins)

1 small head cauliflower, broken into large florets

1 red bell pepper, sliced

2 teaspoons salt

1½ cups chicken stock

1 cup frozen peas

1 cup unsweetened coconut milk

salt and freshly ground black pepper

¼ cup shredded fresh basil

1. Pre-heat the pressure cooker using the BROWN setting.

2. Add the oil and butter and cook the onion, garlic and ginger until tender. Add the curry powder, cayenne pepper and tomato paste, and stir to combine well. Cook for another minute to toast the spices. Add the chicken, apple, raisins, cauliflower, red pepper and salt, and stir well to coat. Pour in the chicken stock and lock the lid in place.

3. Pressure cook on HIGH for 4 minutes.

4. Reduce the pressure with the QUICK-RELEASE method and carefully remove the lid.

5. Keep the curry at a simmer using the BROWN setting. Stir the frozen peas and coconut milk into the curry and season to taste with salt and pepper. Serve with white rice and garnish with shredded basil.

Did You Know....?

Gingerroot keeps very well in the freezer. Try grating it first and then freezing it in small quantities. Then you'll have grated ginger at your fingertips whenever you need it.

Jerk Spiced Chicken Legs with Rice

These chicken legs are so tasty, with a spiciness that warms rather than burns. If you'd like a spicier dish, toss a halved Habañero pepper into the cooker before pressure-cooking. Just remember to remove it before serving!

Serves
4

Cooking Time
8 Minutes

Release Method
Quick-release

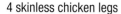

4 skinless chicken legs

2 teaspoons ground allspice

1 teaspoon dried thyme

1 teaspoon ground cinnamon

1 teaspoon paprika

2 teaspoons ground nutmeg

1 teaspoon ground ginger

2 teaspoons chili powder

pinch cayenne pepper

2 teaspoons salt

2 tablespoons vegetable oil

1 onion, finely chopped

1½ cups long-grain white rice

2½ cups chicken stock

1 teaspoon salt

¼ cup chopped fresh cilantro (or parsley)

1. If your chicken legs are very large, separate them into thighs and drumsticks. Otherwise, leave them whole. Combine the next 9 ingredients for the jerk spice rub. Rub the spice mix all over the chicken legs, or combine the spice mix and chicken legs in a plastic zipper lock bag and shake around until the legs are evenly coated. If you have time, leave the chicken with the rub for up to 30 minutes. Otherwise, proceed with the recipe.

2. Pre-heat the pressure cooker using the BROWN setting.

3. Add 1 tablespoon of the oil to the cooker and sear the chicken legs until well browned on all sides. Remove to a side plate and reserve. Add the remaining oil to the cooker and cook the onion until tender. Add the rice and stir to coat with the oil. Add the chicken stock and salt and then return the chicken legs to the cooker, placing them on top of the rice. Lock the lid in place.

4. Pressure cook on HIGH for 8 minutes.

5. Reduce the pressure with the QUICK-RELEASE method and carefully remove the lid.

6. Remove the chicken to a side plate and fluff the rice with a fork. Serve the chicken and rice together and sprinkle with chopped cilantro.

Cilantro will store for up to a week in the refrigerator if you place the stems in a glass of water and cover the top with a plastic bag.

Chicken and Lemon-Chive Dumplings

Chicken and Dumplings just screams comfort food no matter which type of dumpling is involved – the flat rolled dumpling, or the fluffy dropped dumpling. I prefer the dropped dumpling, probably because that's what my mother made when I was a child. Adding the lemon zest and chives to the dumpling batter lightens and brightens the dumplings just a little. The dumplings actually cook on top of the piping hot chicken stew at the very end of cooking.

Serves
6

Cooking Time
10 Minutes

Release Method
Quick-release

2 tablespoons olive oil

1 onion, chopped

2 ribs celery, chopped

2 carrots, chopped (about 1 cup)

2 cloves garlic, smashed

1 teaspoon dried thyme

½ teaspoon dried rosemary

½ cup white wine or dry vermouth

4 cups good quality chicken stock

3 cups diced red-skinned potatoes (about 1 pound)

1½ pounds boneless skinless chicken breasts and thighs, cut into bite-sized pieces

2 teaspoons salt

freshly ground black pepper

1½ cups Bisquick® mix

½ cup milk

6 tablespoons chopped fresh chives

2 tablespoons lemon zest (about 2 lemons)

¼ cup butter, softened at room temperature

½ cup flour

¼ cup heavy cream

¼ chopped fresh parsley

1. Pre-heat the pressure cooker using the BROWN setting.

2. Add the olive oil to the cooker and sauté the onion, celery and carrots until they start to become tender – about 5 minutes. Add the garlic and dried spices and cook for another 2 minutes. Add the white wine (or vermouth), chicken stock, potatoes and chicken pieces. Season with salt and freshly ground black pepper, give everything a good stir and lock the lid in place.

3. Pressure cook on HIGH for 10 minutes.

4. While the stew is cooking, make your dumplings. Combine the Bisquick® mix with the milk, chives and lemon zest in a bowl and stir until the dough forms. Set aside.

5. In a second bowl, combine the butter and flour to form a paste (called a beurre manié) and set aside.

6. Release the pressure using the QUICK-RELEASE method and carefully remove the lid. Ladle some of the hot liquid from the cooker into the bowl with the beurre manié and whisk well. Pour the mixture back into the cooker, and add the cream and parsley. Return the cooker to the BROWN setting and bring everything to a gentle simmer. Season to taste with salt and freshly ground black pepper.

7. Drop dumplings the size of golf balls onto the surface of the stew. Let the stew simmer for a couple of minutes. Then, put the lid on the cooker, turn it off and let the chicken and dumplings sit for at least 10 minutes before serving.

If you don't want to open a whole bottle of wine for a recipe, substituting vermouth is a good idea. An open bottle of vermouth keeps for about three months when stored in the refrigerator. Substitute dry vermouth for white wine, and sweet vermouth for red wine.

Whole Chicken with Marinara and Vegetables

This is a meal you can throw together in a hurry if you've forgotten about dinner. Just pick up a whole chicken and a jar of marinara sauce at the grocery store and add whatever vegetables you have in the fridge. Dinner will be done in just half an hour!

Serves
2 to 4

Cooking Time
25 Minutes

Release Method
Natural-release

1 teaspoon salt

1 teaspoon ground paprika

freshly ground black pepper

1 (3-pound) chicken

olive oil

1 onion, cut into large chunks

1 red pepper, cut into large chunks

1 green pepper, cut into large chunks

1 clove garlic, smashed

1 teaspoon dried oregano

2 tablespoons tomato paste

1 (24-ounce) jar marinara sauce

1 cup chicken stock

½ cup heavy cream (optional)

¼ cup chopped fresh parsley or basil

1. Pre-heat the pressure cooker using the BROWN setting.

2. Combine the salt, paprika and freshly ground black pepper and rub this mix all over the chicken and inside the cavity. Add olive oil to the cooker and brown the chicken breast side down (if you're in a rush, you can skip this step but the chicken won't look as nice). Remove the chicken and set it aside.

3. Add a little more oil to the cooker and sauté the onion until the onion starts to soften – about 5 minutes. Add peppers, garlic, oregano and tomato paste, and cook for another minute or two. Pour in the marinara sauce and chicken stock, scraping the bottom of the cooker to pick up any brown bits that may have accumulated there. Return the chicken to the cooker and nestle it breast side down into the sauce. Lock the lid in place.

4. Pressure cook on HIGH for 25 minutes.

5. Let the pressure drop NATURALLY and carefully remove the lid. Remove the chicken to a serving plate. Let the marinara and vegetables sit for a minute or two and then spoon off any extra fat that rises to the top and discard. For a creamy sauce, stir in the heavy cream and season to taste with salt and freshly ground black pepper. Pour the sauce and vegetables over the chicken and sprinkle the chopped parsley or basil on top.

The skin of the chicken will not brown or crisp up in the pressure cooker. If you don't want to eat the skin, you can choose to remove the skin before rubbing on the spice blend and browning it, or you can simply pull the skin off the chicken at the end of cooking.

Chicken Breasts Florentine with Mushrooms

Any recipe in Florentine style refers to spinach as one of the main ingredients, and that's exactly what we have here – an elegant dinner for two with beautiful baby spinach and mushrooms in a cream sauce poured over sliced chicken breasts. This can easily be doubled for four people, just place the browned chicken breasts on their sides next to each other when you return them to the cooker.

Serves
2

Cooking Time
2 Minutes

Release Method
Natural-release

2 tablespoons olive oil

2 boneless, skinless chicken breasts

salt and freshly ground black pepper

1 onion, finely chopped

1 clove garlic, minced

4 ounces brown mushrooms, sliced

salt and freshly ground black pepper

½ cup chicken stock

½ cup heavy cream

1 tablespoon butter, softened

1 tablespoon flour

3 ounces baby spinach (about 3 cups packed)

1. Pre-heat the pressure cooker using the BROWN setting.

2. Add the oil to the cooker and brown the chicken breasts well on both sides, seasoning with salt and freshly ground black pepper. Set the browned chicken breasts aside and add the onion, garlic and mushrooms to the cooker. Sauté until the vegetables start to soften – about 5 minutes. Add the chicken stock and cream and return the chicken breasts to the cooker. Lock the lid in place.

3. Pressure cook on HIGH for 2 minutes.

4. While the chicken is cooking, combine the butter and flour in a small bowl until it forms a paste (called a beurre manié).

5. Let the pressure drop NATURALLY and carefully remove the lid. Remove the chicken breasts and set aside. Stir the spinach into the mushrooms and onions, letting it wilt. Return the cooker to the BROWN setting and stir in the beurre manié vigorously. Bring the sauce to a simmer to thicken and season to taste with salt and pepper. Slice the chicken breasts on the bias and spoon the spinach and mushrooms over the top.

Chicken Tikka Masala

Though it didn't actually originate in India, Chicken Tikka Masala is a classic Indian take out dinner. It is said to be of British origin, but it has become one of the most popular items ordered at Indian restaurants worldwide. Chunks of chicken are marinated in yogurt and then cooked in a spicy sauce. It's one of my favorites, no matter where it originated!

Serves
4 to 6

Cooking Time
3 Minutes

Release Method
Natural-release

½ cup plain yogurt (regular or low-fat, but not Greek yogurt)

1 tablespoon ground coriander

2 teaspoons ground cumin

2 teaspoons garam masala

1 tablespoon turmeric

1 teaspoon smoked paprika

pinch of cayenne pepper (according to taste)

2 teaspoons salt

2 pounds boneless, skinless chicken breasts or thighs, cut into 2-inch strips

2 tablespoons butter

1 onion, finely chopped

2 cloves garlic, minced

1 tablespoon grated fresh ginger

1 (28-ounce) can tomatoes, chopped

2 tablespoons tomato paste

½ cup heavy cream

½ cup water

cilantro leaves, for garnish

1. Combine the yogurt, spices and salt in a bowl, add the chicken and marinate for an hour.

2. Pre-heat the pressure cooker using the BROWN setting.

3. Add the butter to the cooker and sauté the onion, garlic and ginger for a few minutes. Add the chicken and the marinade and stir for another 30 to 60 seconds. Add the tomatoes, tomato paste, heavy cream and water and stir well. Lock the lid in place.

4. Pressure cook on HIGH for 3 minutes.

5. Let the pressure drop NATURALLY and carefully remove the lid. Stir in the fresh cilantro leaves and serve over rice.

Fresh ginger freezes really well. Grate it first and then freeze it in tablespoon-sized portions. Then, you'll always have some ready when you need it.

Beef

Beef Bolognese

Beef, Rice and Cabbage Casserole

Swiss Steak

Osso Bucco

Hungarian Beef Goulash

Corned Beef with Potatoes and Cabbage

Beef Bourguignon

Classic Pot Roast

Sweet Vidalia Onion Joes

Hunter's Beef Stew

Beef Dip Sandwiches

Braised Beef Short Ribs

Dijon and Thyme Meatloaf with Caramelized Onions

Beef Bolognese

Few things can get my mouth watering faster than a bowl of pasta with Bolognese sauce... especially when this version only takes 10 minutes of cooking time!

Serves
4

Cooking Time
10 Minutes

Release Method
Quick-release

1 pound ground beef

½ pound ground pork

1 onion, finely chopped

2 cloves garlic, minced

2 carrots, finely chopped

2 ribs of celery, finely chopped

1 teaspoon dried oregano

1 bay leaf

4 sprigs fresh thyme

½ cup red wine

1 (28 ounce) can whole tomatoes

2 tablespoons tomato paste

½ cup beef stock

2 teaspoons salt

freshly ground black pepper

½ cup grated Parmesan cheese

1. Pre-heat the pressure cooker using the BROWN setting.

2. Brown beef and pork in batches until the meat has broken up and the fat has been rendered. Set the browned meat aside and pour off all but one tablespoon of the fat.

3. Add the onion, garlic, carrots and celery to the cooker and cook for a few minutes. Stir in the dried oregano, bay leaf and fresh thyme and cook for another minute or two. Stir in the red wine, tomatoes, tomato paste, beef stock and salt and pepper. Return the meat to the cooker and lock the lid in place.

4. Pressure cook on HIGH for 10 minutes.

5. Release the pressure using the QUICK-RELEASE method and carefully remove the lid.

6. Season to taste with salt and freshly ground black pepper and stir in the Parmesan cheese.

Whole canned tomatoes generally have a better flavor than diced tomatoes, so choose whole tomatoes and then break them up in the sauce as you stir.

Beef, Rice and Cabbage Casserole

*This is a hearty meal that will keep you satisfied for a long time. I think of it as peasant food –
accessible, inexpensive ingredients that are spiced up into something very pleasing.*

Serves
4 to 6

Cooking Time
6 Minutes

Release Method
Natural-release

1 tablespoon olive oil

1 pound ground beef

1 onion, chopped

1 clove garlic, sliced

2 teaspoons salt

freshly ground black pepper

1 teaspoon dried thyme

1 teaspoon dried oregano

½ teaspoon smoked paprika

1 tablespoon red wine vinegar

1 tablespoon tomato paste

1 tablespoon brown sugar

1 (28-ounce) can tomatoes

1 (14-ounce) can crushed tomatoes

½ cup raisins

½ cup basmati rice

4 cups coarsely chopped green cabbage
(about ⅓ to ½ head)

2 cups beef stock

¼ cup chopped fresh parsley

1. Pre-heat the pressure cooker using the BROWN setting.

2. Add the oil to the cooker and brown the beef, breaking it up as you do so. Remove the beef from the cooker with a slotted spoon and set aside. Drain off all but one tablespoon of the fat. Add the onion, garlic and spices, and cook for a few minutes.

3. Add the vinegar, tomato paste and brown sugar and cook, stirring for another minute. Stir in the tomatoes, raisins, rice and cabbage, return the beef to the cooker and combine well. Add the stock and push the ingredients down into the liquid.

4. Pressure cook on HIGH for 6 minutes.

5. Let the pressure drop NATURALLY and carefully remove the lid. Sprinkle the fresh parsley over the top.

Swiss Steak

As with so many dishes that have a country's name in the title, this dish of steak, pounded flat, seared and then braised in a tomato- based sauce is not Swiss in origin. The name actually comes from the word "swissing" which is a method smoothing out fabric between rollers, making it flat.

Serves
4

Cooking Time
25 Minutes

Release Method
Natural-release

2 pounds top beef round, cut into ½-inch steaks and pounded flat

salt and freshly ground black pepper

2 tablespoons olive oil

2 ribs celery, sliced 1-inch thick

2 carrots, sliced 1-inch thick

2 onions, sliced

1 clove garlic, minced

1 tablespoon prepared horseradish

1 (8-ounce) can tomato sauce

¾ cup beef broth, divided

1 bay leaf

¼ cup flour (optional)

¼ cup chopped fresh parsley

1. Pre-heat the pressure cooker using the BROWN setting.

2. Season the beef with salt and freshly ground black pepper. Add the oil to the cooker and brown the steaks on both sides. Add the celery, carrots, onion, garlic, horseradish, tomato sauce, beef broth and the bay leaf. Lock the lid in place.

3. Pressure cook on HIGH for 25 minutes.

4. Let the pressure drop NATURALLY and carefully remove the lid. Transfer the meat to a plate to rest.

5. Return the cooker to the BROWN setting and bring the sauce up to a simmer. To thicken the sauce, remove a quarter cup of the cooking liquid and whisk it together with the flour in a separate bowl. Stir this mixture back into the simmering sauce to thicken it. Return the meat to the sauce and let it re-heat for a minute. Serve over egg noodles or rice with fresh parsley sprinkled over the top.

Osso Bucco

"Osso Bucco" comes from the Italian for "bone with a hole", in reference to the veal shanks used in the dish. It's usually served over risotto Milanese, but can be made with egg noodles or potatoes as an accompaniment. To me, Osso Bucco is a special occasion meal that usually takes a few hours. Now, with the pressure cooker, it can be done in about 30 minutes!

Serves
4

Cooking Time
30 Minutes

Release Method
Natural-release

4 large veal shanks

salt and freshly ground black pepper

flour for dredging

1 to 2 tablespoons olive oil

1 onion, finely chopped

2 carrots, sliced ¼-inch thick

2 ribs of celery, sliced ¼-inch thick

2 teaspoons fresh thyme leaves

1 bay leaf

1 teaspoon dried oregano

½ cup red wine

1 (14 ounce) can diced tomatoes

1 cup beef stock

For the *gremolata*:

zest of 1 orange, finely chopped

2 cloves garlic, minced

2 tablespoons chopped fresh parsley

1. Pre-heat the pressure cooker using the BROWN setting.

2. Season the veal shanks with salt and pepper and dredge them lightly in flour, shaking off any excess. Add the oil to the cooker and brown the shanks on all sides. Remove the browned shanks to a plate and set aside.

3. Add the onion, carrots and celery to the cooker and cook for a few minutes. Add the thyme, bay leaf and oregano and cook for another minute or so. Add the wine and using a wooden spoon, scrape up any brown bits that have formed on the bottom of the cooker while you bring the liquid to a simmer. Add the tomatoes and beef stock and return the veal to the cooker. Lock the lid in place.

4. Pressure cook on HIGH for 30 minutes. While the veal is cooking, make the gremolata by chopping the orange zest, garlic and parsley and combining in a small bowl.

5. Let the pressure drop NATURALLY and carefully remove the lid.

6. Season the sauce to taste with salt and pepper and serve over polenta or risotto with the gremolata sprinkled on top.

Hungarian Beef Goulash

Serves
6

Cooking Time
15 Minutes

Release Method
Natural-release

4 slices bacon, chopped

2 pounds boneless beef shank or chuck, cut into ½-inch pieces

1 onion, finely chopped

2 cloves garlic, minced

1 teaspoon caraway seeds

3 tablespoons Hungarian sweet paprika

½ cup white wine

1 (14 ounce) can diced tomatoes (fire-roasted recommended)

½ cup jarred or canned roasted red peppers, diced

1 russet potato, peeled and cut into chunks

½ cup beef stock

1½ teaspoons salt

freshly ground black pepper

½ cup chopped fresh parsley

1. Pre-heat the pressure cooker using the BROWN setting.

2. Cook the bacon until crispy, then remove and set aside to use for another purpose. Drain all but 1 tablespoon of fat from the cooker. Brown the beef in batches. Remove the browned beef to a plate and set aside.

3. Add the onion, garlic and caraway seeds to the cooker and cook for a few minutes. Add the paprika and cook for another minute or so. Add the white wine and using a wooden spoon, scrape up any brown bits that have formed on the bottom of the cooker. Add the tomatoes, roasted peppers, potato, beef stock and salt and pepper, and return the beef to the cooker. Lock the lid in place.

4. Pressure cook on HIGH for 15 minutes.

5. Let pressure drop NATURALLY and carefully remove the lid.

6. Stir the goulash well as you mix in the parsley. This will break the potato a little and thicken the goulash. Season to taste with salt and pepper and serve over mashed potatoes or egg noodles.

Did You Know...?

Just as with the Chicken Paprikash, this Hungarian Goulash gets much of its flavor from the paprika included. Hungarians take their paprika seriously, and Hungarian paprika is considered to be the finest in the world. So, once again, I highly recommend getting the best Hungarian paprika that you can find.

Corned Beef with Potatoes and Cabbage

The only downside to corned beef and cabbage is that most of us only have it once a year! Now that you no longer need the entire afternoon to simmer the beef, maybe you can enjoy it more often.

Serves
3 to 6

Cooking Time
55 + 3 Minutes

Release Method
Natural-release

3-pound corned beef brisket

2 teaspoons black peppercorns

1 cinnamon stick, broken in half

4 allspice berries

3 whole cloves

2 bay leaves

3 cloves garlic, peeled and smashed

1 white onion, peeled and sliced

6 red potatoes, scrubbed and sliced
½-inch thick

1 head green cabbage, cut into wedges

1 to 2 tablespoons butter

1 tablespoon fresh thyme leaves

1. Place a rack in the bottom of the pressure cooker. Rinse the corned beef under cool water and then place it on the rack, fat side up. Pour water into the cooker so that it just covers the beef. Add the peppercorns, cinnamon stick, allspice berries, cloves, bay leaves, and garlic to the liquid and scatter the onions on top of the beef. Lock the lid in place.

2. Pressure cook on HIGH for 55 minutes.

3. Let the pressure drop NATURALLY and carefully remove the lid.

4. Transfer the corned beef to a resting platter and loosely tent it with foil. Add the potatoes and cabbage to the liquid in the cooker and lock the lid in place again.

5. Pressure cook on HIGH for 3 minutes.

6. Reduce the pressure with the QUICK-RELEASE method and carefully remove the lid.

7. Transfer the potatoes and cabbage to a serving dish with a slotted spoon. Toss the vegetables with the butter and fresh thyme and serve along with the corned beef, sliced against the grain into ½-inch slices.

When buying a corned beef, you'll have two different cuts to choose from. The *point cut* has more fat, but also more flavor. Estimate about a pound per person of a point cut corned beef. The *flat cut* has less fat and is easier to slice. Your yield will be higher with a flat cut, so estimate about ½ to ¾ pound of flat cut corned beef per person. For a darker brisket with slightly charred, crispy edges, broil the cooked brisket under the broiler for a minute or two before slicing and serving.

Beef Bourguignon

This recipe really benefits from sautéing the mushrooms and pearl onions separately and then adding them to the dish at the end. Of course, if you don't have the time or energy for this extra step, just add the onions and mushrooms to the pot before pressure cooking.

Serves
4 to 6

Cooking Time
15 Minutes

Release Method
Natural-release

4 ounces bacon, chopped

1½ pounds beef round or chuck roast, cut into 2-inch pieces

salt and freshly ground black pepper

1 shallot, finely chopped

2 cloves of garlic, minced

1 rib of celery, sliced ½-inch thick

2 carrots, cut into 2-inch pieces

1 bay leaf

1½ teaspoons dried thyme

2 tablespoons tomato paste

1 bottle Pinot Noir wine

1 to 2 cups beef stock

3 tablespoons butter, divided

16 pearl onions, peeled
(or use frozen, thawed)

12 ounces crimini or shiitake mushrooms, stems removed and halved

1 to 2 teaspoons chopped fresh thyme leaves

2 tablespoons flour

fresh rosemary sprigs, for garnish

1. Pre-heat the pressure cooker using the BROWN setting.

2. Add the bacon to the cooker and cook until almost crispy and set aside. Season the beef with salt and pepper, add to the cooker and brown in batches. Remove the browned beef to a plate and set aside.

3. Add the shallot, garlic and celery to the cooker and cook for a few minutes. Add the carrots, bay leaf, thyme and tomato paste and cook for another minute or so. Pour in the wine and using a wooden spoon, scrape up any brown bits that have formed on the bottom of the cooker. Return the beef to the cooker and add enough beef stock to just cover the other ingredients. Lock the lid in place.

4. Pressure cook on HIGH for 15 minutes. While the stew is cooking, heat a skillet over medium-high heat. Melt 1 tablespoon of butter in the pan and cook the pearl onions until they start to brown. Add the mushrooms and thyme and continue to cook until the vegetables are tender. Set aside.

5. Let the pressure drop NATURALLY and carefully remove the lid.

6. Combine the remaining two tablespoons of butter with the flour in a small bowl to make a paste. Bring the stew to a simmer using the BROWN setting and stir the butter and flour paste into the sauce to thicken it. Season to taste with salt and pepper. Return the bacon to the cooker and add the sautéed onions and mushrooms. Serve over mashed potatoes, noodles or rice and garnish with small rosemary sprigs.

For a more elegant meal, after removing the lid of the pressure cooker in step 6, remove the beef pieces and carrots to a resting plate. Using a fine strainer, strain the sauce into a small saucepan. Bring the sauce to a simmer and whisk the butter and flour paste into the simmering liquid. Season with salt and pepper. Pour this sauce over the beef, carrots, onions, mushrooms and bacon, garnishing with chopped fresh parsley.

Classic Pot Roast

A pot roast is a perfect meal to make in a pressure cooker. You can buy a cheap, but flavorful cut of meat and, in just an hour, serve up a tender roast with delicious gravy. The vegetables in this pot roast cook for the entire duration of the cooking time, and will be very soft at the end. If you prefer your vegetables with some bite to them, use the quick-release method to open the cooker after 35 minutes of cooking the roast, and then add the carrots and potatoes. Then return the cooker to pressure and proceed with the recipe.

Serves
6

Cooking Time
50 Minutes

Release Method
Natural-release

3-pound boneless chuck roast

salt and freshly ground black pepper

1 tablespoon vegetable oil

1 onion, chopped

2 ribs celery, chopped

1 cup red wine

2 cups beef stock

2 to 3 sprigs of fresh thyme

1 bay leaf

3 carrots, sliced into 2-inch slices
(or use 18 baby cut carrots)

8 to 12 fingerling potatoes, left whole

2 tablespoons flour or cornstarch
(optional)

¼ cup chopped fresh parsley

1. Pre-heat the pressure cooker using the BROWN setting.

2. Season the roast on all sides with salt and pepper. Add the oil to the cooker and brown the roast on all sides. Remove the browned roast to a plate and set aside.

3. Add the onion and celery to the cooker and cook for a few minutes. Pour in the red wine and using a wooden spoon, scrape up any brown bits that have formed on the bottom while you bring the liquid to a simmer. Add the beef stock, thyme and bay leaf and return the roast to the cooker. Scatter the carrots and potatoes on top and lock the lid in place.

4. Pressure cook on HIGH for 50 minutes.

5. Let the pressure drop NATURALLY and carefully remove the lid.

6. Transfer the roast and vegetables to a plate and tent with foil. Bring the sauce to a simmer using the BROWN setting and let it reduce for about 10 minutes while the roast rests. If you'd like thicker gravy, mix the 2 tablespoons of flour or cornstarch with 2 tablespoons of water and stir the mixture into the sauce. Season to taste with salt and pepper and spoon the liquid and vegetables over the roast. Garnish with chopped fresh parsley.

Did You Know...?

Mixing equal parts cornstarch and cold water together is called making a slurry. A slurry can be used to thicken any liquid, but the liquid must be brought to a boil in order to thicken. Don't boil it for too long, however, because the cornstarch will break down and the liquid will thin out again.

Sweet Vidalia Onion Joes

This, of course, is a riff on traditional Sloppy Joes, adding sweet Vidalia onion to the mix, along with a little brown sugar and the secret ingredient – balsamic vinegar. The result is a slightly sweeter version of a dish everyone of my age remembers enjoying as a kid.

Serves
4 to 6

Cooking Time
10 Minutes

Release Method
Combo

1½ pounds lean ground beef

1 tablespoon vegetable oil

1 large Vidalia (or other sweet) onion, finely chopped

2 cloves garlic, minced

1 teaspoon dried oregano

2 tablespoons brown sugar

1 tablespoon balsamic vinegar

2 tablespoons tomato ketchup

1 (14-ounce) can tomatoes, chopped or crushed by hand

½ cup beef stock

1 teaspoon salt

freshly ground black pepper

4 to 6 Kaiser rolls, Ciabatta, hamburger buns or potato rolls

1. Pre-heat the pressure cooker using the BROWN setting.

2. Brown the beef, stirring to break the ground beef up into small pieces. Transfer the beef to a bowl with a slotted spoon, draining away and discarding all the fat.

3. Add the oil to the cooker, sauté the onion, garlic and oregano and cook until the onion starts to soften and brown slightly – about 8 minutes. Add the brown sugar, balsamic vinegar, tomato ketchup and tomatoes and stir well. Return the beef to the cooker, pour in the beef stock, season with salt and freshly ground black pepper and lock the lid in place.

4. Pressure cook on HIGH for 10 minutes.

5. Let the pressure drop NATURALLY for 10 minutes. Release any residual pressure with the QUICK-RELEASE method and carefully remove the lid. Season to taste again with salt and freshly ground black pepper and serve over the bread rolls.

 Did You Know...?

The secret to a good Sloppy Joe rests with the bun you choose to put underneath. The bun should definitely absorb all the juice and flavor from the meat, but you also want it to hold its shape somewhat, and not disintegrate. I prefer a Ciabatta or Kaiser roll, but hamburger buns or potato rolls will do the job too.

Hunter's Beef Stew

This recipe is really a version of beef Cacciatore – Italian for "hunter". It's an earthy stew with mushrooms, peppers and carrots, but what makes it really special is the horseradish that is stirred in at the end, giving it a "je ne sais quoi" quality.

Serves
4

Cooking Time
20 Minutes

Release Method
Natural-release

1 tablespoon vegetable oil

2 pounds beef stew meat, trimmed of fat and cut into bite-sized pieces

salt and freshly ground black pepper

1 onion, chopped into ½-inch pieces

2 carrots, chopped into 1-inch chunks (about 2 cups)

2 cloves garlic, minced

1 green bell pepper, chopped into 1-inch chunks

1 red bell pepper, chopped into 1-inch chunks

8 ounces button mushrooms, quartered

1 teaspoon dried thyme

1 sprig of fresh rosemary

½ cup red wine

1½ cups beef stock

2 tablespoons Worcestershire sauce

1 (14-ounce) can of tomatoes, diced

2 tablespoons prepared horseradish (not horseradish sauce)

fresh thyme, for garnish

1. Pre-heat the pressure cooker using the BROWN setting.

2. Add the oil to the cooker and brown the beef in batches, seasoning with salt and pepper and setting the browned beef aside in a bowl. Add the onions and carrots to the cooker and sauté until the onion starts to become tender – about 5 minutes. Add the garlic, peppers, mushrooms, thyme and rosemary and stir well. Cook for an additional minute or two. Pour in the red wine, beef stock, Worcestershire sauce and tomatoes, and bring to a boil. Return the beef to the cooker and stir well, doing your best to submerge the beef in the liquid. Lock the lid in place.

3. Pressure cook on HIGH for 20 minutes.

4. Let the pressure drop NATURALLY and carefully remove the lid. Stir in the horseradish and season to taste with salt and freshly ground black pepper. Don't forget to remove the sprig of rosemary before serving with some fresh thyme leaves on top.

Prepared horseradish in its most basic form is made of the grated horseradish root and distilled vinegar. Different manufacturers then add seasonings and sometimes cream. I prefer a basic horseradish for this recipe, but you should use the variety you like best.

Beef Dip Sandwiches

When I was a kid, I LOVED a beef dip sandwich and can remember ordering it many times on those occasions when I was out to lunch with my mum. It's the simplest of sandwiches, but somehow it's made fun by having the jus to dip the sandwich in. It's not just a kid thing though, because I still love a good beef dip sandwich today!

Serves
8

Cooking Time
35 Minutes

Release Method
Natural-release

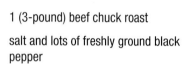

1 (3-pound) beef chuck roast

salt and lots of freshly ground black pepper

2 tablespoons olive oil

3 onions, thinly sliced

2 cloves garlic, smashed

1 teaspoon brown sugar

1 teaspoon dried thyme

½ teaspoon dried rosemary

1 bay leaf

3 cups good quality beef stock

8 white Italian bread rolls

½ cup horseradish

¼ cup sour cream

1. Pre-heat the pressure cooker using the BROWN setting.

2. Season the beef roast with salt and pepper. Add the oil and brown the beef well on all sides. Take some time with this step and try not to be impatient. Remove the roast to a side plate. Add the onion, garlic, brown sugar and dried herbs and cook until the onions start to brown. Add a little beef stock, stir and continue to brown until the onions are golden – about 15 minutes. Pour in the remaining beef stock, scraping the bottom of the cooker to stir up any of the brown bits, and return the roast to the cooker. Lock the lid in place.

3. Pressure cook on HIGH for 35 minutes.

4. Let the pressure drop NATURALLY and carefully remove the lid. Remove the roast to a resting plate and loosely tent with foil for at least 10 minutes. While the roast is resting, return the cooker to the BROWN setting and let the onion jus reduce to concentrate the flavors. Season to taste with salt and pepper. Strain the jus into a fat separator and let the fat rise to the surface. Pour the flavorful jus out into ramekins and discard the fat and bay leaf.

5. Combine the horseradish and sour cream and spread the mixture on each side of the rolls. Thinly slice the beef and fill the sandwiches with the beef and onions. Serve each sandwich with a little ramekin of jus for dipping.

Did You Know...?

Having a flavorful jus is critical to the success of this simple sandwich. So, use the best quality beef stock you can. You can also fortify the stock by adding beef bones to the liquid as it simmers and cooks the beef.

Braised Beef Short Ribs

Anyone with a pressure cooker should have a basic recipe for short ribs. The pressure cooker makes quick work of them, turning them into decadent chunks of tender rib.

Serves
4

Cooking Time
55 Minutes

Release Method
Natural-release

3 pounds beef short ribs

¼ cup flour

2 tablespoons olive oil

1 large onion, chopped

2 carrots, chopped

2 ribs celery, chopped

½ cup red wine

1 (14-ounce) can diced tomatoes

2 cups beef stock

2 tablespoons Worcestershire sauce

1 bay leaf

⅓ cup instant potato flakes

salt and freshly ground black pepper

¼ cup chopped fresh parsley

1. Pre-heat the pressure cooker using the BROWN setting.

2. Season the short ribs with salt and pepper and dredge them lightly in flour. Add the olive oil to the cooker and brown short ribs on all sides. You will have to do this in batches. Set the browned ribs aside on a resting plate.

3. Add the onions to the cooker and sauté until they start to brown – about 8 to 10 minutes. Add the carrots and celery and cook for a few more minutes until the vegetables start to soften. Deglaze the cooker by pouring in the red wine and scraping any brown bits from the bottom of the insert. Stir in the diced tomatoes, beef stock and Worcestershire sauce. Return the ribs to cooker nestling them into vegetables and liquid and lock the lid in place.

4. Pressure cook on HIGH for 55 minutes.

5. Let pressure drop NATURALLY and carefully remove the lid. Remove ribs from cooker and place on a plate, tenting with aluminum foil to keep them warm. Let the braising liquid sit for a minute or two and then skim the fat off the top of the sauce with a ladle or large spoon.

6. Return the pressure cooker to the BROWN setting and stir in the potato flakes. Bring the liquid to a simmer, stirring while the sauce thickens. Season with salt and pepper. Serve the ribs and sauce together over mashed potatoes or polenta, with parsley sprinkled on top.

There are two types of beef short ribs, depending on how they are cut by the butcher. "English Style" short ribs are cut parallel to the bone so they have one long rib bone covered with meat. "Flanken Style" short ribs are cut across the bones, creating a piece of meat that has three or four little bones in it. Either cut is suitable for this recipe although the Flanken Style will fit more easily into a smaller cooker.

Dijon and Thyme Meatloaf with Caramelized Onions

It's always fun to incorporate a new flavor into something traditional. Here, Dijon mustard and fresh thyme adds just that little variation into one of America's favorite dinners – meatloaf.

Serves
6 to 8

Cooking Time
35 Minutes

Release Method
Natural-release

Meatloaf:

2 pounds lean ground beef

1 cup panko breadcrumbs

½ onion, finely chopped

½ cup Dijon mustard

1 egg, lightly beaten

2 tablespoons fresh thyme leaves

3 tablespoons Worcestershire sauce

1 teaspoon salt

freshly ground black ground pepper

1½ cups beef stock

Glaze:

¾ cup ketchup

¼ cup Dijon mustard

1 tablespoon dark brown sugar

1 teaspoon Worcestershire sauce

Caramelized Onions:

¼ cup butter

1½ onions, chopped

2 tablespoons dark brown sugar

1. In a large bowl, combine the ground beef, breadcrumbs, finely chopped onion, Dijon mustard, egg, thyme, Worcestershire sauce, salt and pepper, and mix together (your hands are great a great tool for this) until everything is combined.

2. Spread a piece a large piece of aluminum foil out on the counter about 20 inches long. Transfer the meatloaf mixture to the middle of the foil and shape into a round form that will fit in your pressure cooker. Fold the aluminum foil loosely up around the sides meatloaf, leaving the top open. Poke a few holes around the perimeter of the foil around the meatloaf (this is for the fat to drain away from the meatloaf). Place a rack in the pressure cooker and pour the beef stock in the bottom. Holding onto the ends of the foil, lower the meatloaf onto the rack in the cooker.

3. In a small bowl, mix together the glaze ingredients until combined. Spread the glaze on top of meatloaf, letting some of it drip down the sides of the meatloaf. Lock the lid in place.

4. Pressure cook on HIGH for 35 minutes.

5. While the meatloaf is cooking, prepare the caramelized onions. Melt the butter in a large saucepan over medium high heat. Add the onions, cook for 2 minutes and then add the dark brown sugar. Reduce the temperature to low heat and continue to cook for about 15 minutes, stirring often. Deglaze the pan with ¼ cup water, scraping up all the browning on the bottom of the pan, and continue to cook until the onions are soft and browned. Then keep them warm over very low heat.

6. Let the pressure drop NATURALLY and carefully remove the lid. Use the foil to carefully remove the meatloaf from the cooker and transfer it to serving platter, top with the caramelized onions and slice up to serve.

Pork

Dry-Rubbed Baby Back Ribs with BBQ Sauce

Italian Sausage with White Beans and Roasted Red Pepper

Country Style Pork Ribs with Mustard and Cream

Pork Carnitas

Pork Stew with Cabbage and Tomatoes

Asian Country-Style Pork Ribs

Gumbo and Rice

Braised Pork Shoulder with Sauerkraut

Apple Stuffed Pork Chops

Asian Meatballs

Dry-Rubbed Baby Back Ribs with BBQ Sauce

This is my favorite method of cooking ribs in the pressure cooker. The spice rub applied to the ribs before browning gives them color and flavor and steaming the ribs over a flavorful broth makes them super tender without washing away the flavor. The finishing touch is transforming the flavorful broth into a sauce to slather on the ribs at the end.

Serves
4

Cooking Time
30 Minutes

Release Method
Natural-release

2 teaspoons smoked paprika

1 teaspoon dry mustard powder

2 teaspoons dried oregano

2 teaspoons dried thyme

1 teaspoon chili powder

2 teaspoons salt

3 pounds baby back ribs (about 2 racks), cut into 3-rib sections

1 to 2 tablespoons olive or vegetable oil

½ onion, chopped

1 bay leaf

1 cup beef stock

Sauce:

1 cup tomato ketchup

2 tablespoons molasses

1 tablespoon cider vinegar

1 tablespoon tomato paste

½ teaspoon soy sauce

1. Combine the first 6 ingredients to make the dry rub spice blend, and rub the spice blend all over the rib sections.

2. Pre-heat the pressure cooker using the BROWN setting.

3. Add the oil to the cooker and brown the ribs in batches. (Alternately, you can do this in a pan on the stovetop.) Remove the ribs and set aside. Add the onion and bay leaf to the cooker and sauté until the onion starts to soften – about 5 minutes. Pour in the beef stock and place a steam rack in the bottom of the cooker. Place the browned ribs on the rack, and lock the lid in place. It's ok to pile the ribs on top of each other in an uneven manner, or to stand the ribs up vertically.

4. Pressure cook on HIGH for 30 minutes.

5. While the ribs are cooking, combine the ketchup, molasses, cider vinegar, tomato paste and soy sauce in a small bowl.

6. Let the pressure drop NATURALLY and carefully remove the lid. Remove the ribs and let them rest on a side plate. While the ribs are resting, remove the steam rack and pour the ketchup mixture into the cooker with the cooking liquid. Return the cooker to the BROWN setting. Simmer the sauce ingredients for about 5 minutes and then return the ribs to the sauce to coat and serve.

Baby back ribs are leaner and more tender than spare ribs. They are also shorter and fit more easily into most pressure cookers. You can absolutely try this rib-cooking technique with spare ribs, however. Just increase the cooking time to 45 minutes.

Italian Sausage with White Beans and Roasted Red Peppers

The flavor of this dish really changes depending on whether you use sweet or hot Italian sausage. So, why not combine both sweet AND hot Italian sausage for the best of both worlds!

Serves
4 to 6

Cooking Time
8 Minutes

Release Method
Quick-release

1 teaspoon vegetable oil

2 pounds sweet or hot Italian sausage, cut in 2-inch chunks

1 large onion, diced

2 cloves garlic, minced

½ cup white wine

2 (15-ounce) cans white beans, drained and rinsed

1 cup diced roasted red peppers

½ cup chicken stock

1 bay leaf

1 teaspoon Italian seasoning

3 sprigs fresh rosemary

¾ cup grated Parmesan cheese

toasted garlic bread (optional for serving)

1 tablespoon chopped fresh rosemary

1. Pre-heat the pressure cooker using the BROWN setting. Add the oil and brown the sausage chunks on all sides. Remove the browned sausage and set aside.

2. Add the onion and garlic to cooker and sauté until the onions start to brown and soften, about 5 to 8 minutes. Add the white wine and stir, scraping up any brown bits on the bottom of the cooker. Add the white beans, roasted red peppers, chicken stock, bay leaf, Italian seasoning and fresh rosemary. Return the browned sausage to the cooker, give everything a good stir and lock the lid in place.

3. Pressure cook on HIGH for 8 minutes.

4. Release pressure using the QUICK-RELEASE method. Return the pressure cooker to the BROWN setting. Remove the rosemary stems and discard. Turn the cooker off and stir in the grated Parmesan cheese. Serve beans and sausage in bowls or over toasted garlic bread. Sprinkle with chopped fresh rosemary to garnish.

It's a lot easier to cut the sausages when they are very cold (or even partially frozen). So, pop them in the freezer for 10 minutes before chopping them up for this recipe.

Country Style Pork Ribs
with Mustard and Cream

Though the name of this recipe sounds rustic, it can actually pass for an elegant dinner. The sauce is a smooth, but relatively thin sauce that coats the ribs nicely and would be delicious over potatoes too. If you'd prefer a thicker gravy-like sauce, simply whisk in some butter and flour mixed together (a beurre manié) at the end.

Serves
4 to 6

Cooking Time
25 Minutes

Release Method
Natural-release

2 teaspoons smoked paprika

1 teaspoon dry mustard powder

2 teaspoons dried thyme

2 teaspoons salt

freshly ground black pepper

3 pounds country style pork ribs

2 tablespoons olive oil

2 shallots, minced

2 cloves garlic, smashed

2 tablespoons apple cider vinegar

½ cup chicken stock

¾ cup heavy cream

2 tablespoons whole-grain mustard

2 tablespoons chopped fresh thyme

salt and freshly ground black pepper

1. Combine the paprika, mustard powder, dried thyme, salt and freshly ground black pepper. Rub this spice mix onto the ribs and set them aside while you prepare the rest of the ingredients (or leave it on to marinate for up to 24 hours).

2. Pre-heat the pressure cooker using the BROWN setting.

3. Add the oil and brown the ribs in batches on all sides. Set the browned ribs aside. Add the shallots and garlic to the cooker and sauté for 2 to 3 minutes. Add the vinegar, stock, cream and mustard, stir well and return the ribs to the liquid. Lock the lid in place.

4. Pressure cook on HIGH for 25 minutes.

5. Let the pressure drop NATURALLY and carefully remove the lid. Transfer the ribs to a resting plate and loosely tent with foil, for at least 5 minutes. Return the pressure cooker to the BROWN setting and bring the sauce to a simmer. Stir in the fresh thyme. Season to taste with salt and freshly ground black pepper and serve over the ribs.

Did You Know...?

Country-style ribs are not actually ribs at all! They are cut from the blade end of the pork loin, near the shoulder. As a result, they don't actually contain any rib bones and are meatier than baby back or spare ribs. They are really more like pork chops.

Pork Carnitas

This is one of my favorite pork recipes. It's delicious and very versatile. For me, a batch of carnitas will last several meals and can be made into quesadillas, burritos, tacos, salads, and even an open-faced sandwich. Skimming off the fat and reducing the braising liquid also makes a terrific sauce to moisten the meat in whatever you choose to make.

Serves
8 to 10

Cooking Time
55 Minutes

Release Method
Natural-release

3 pounds boneless pork shoulder

2 teaspoons dried oregano

1 teaspoon ground cumin

½ teaspoon ground cayenne pepper

½ teaspoon ground coriander

½ teaspoon ground cinnamon

2 teaspoons salt

2 tablespoons vegetable oil, plus more for frying before serving

2 onions, cut into wedges

4 cloves garlic, smashed

2 Jalapeño peppers, sliced (leave the seeds in if you like really spicy foods)

1 cup beef stock

2 large oranges

flour tortillas, salsa, guacamole, grated Cheddar cheese, sour cream, cilantro (for serving)

1. Cut the pork shoulder into chunks that will fit into your pressure cooker. Combine the oregano, cumin, cayenne pepper, coriander, cinnamon and salt and rub the spice mix on the pork chunks.

2. Pre-heat the pressure cooker using the BROWN setting.

3. Add the oil to the cooker and brown the pork chunks on all sides. Remove the browned pork and set aside. Add the onion, garlic and Jalapeño peppers and cook for a minute or two. Return the pork chunks to the cooker and add the beef stock. Cut the oranges in half, squeeze the juice all over the pork chunks and throw the orange halves into the cooker. The pork should only be partially covered in liquid. Lock the lid in place.

4. Pressure cook on HIGH for 55 minutes.

5. Let the pressure drop NATURALLY and carefully remove the lid. Transfer the pork chunks to a resting plate and let them rest for at least 10 minutes. Shred the pork chunks completely, using two forks. Reserve the shredded pork until you are ready to serve.

6. To serve the carnitas, heat a skillet over medium-high heat. Add some oil to the skillet and fry the shredded pork in batches until it has crispy parts. Serve the crisped pork in taco shells or flour tortillas with your favorite toppings – salsa, guacamole, tomatoes, cheese, sour cream and some cilantro.

Did You Know...?

Most of the spicy heat of a Jalapeño is in its seeds. If you like spicy foods, leave the seeds in the recipe. Otherwise, remove the seeds and slice up just the flesh of the chili pepper.

Pork Stew with Cabbage and Tomatoes

This recipe deserves a more inviting name! Pork and cabbage are a classic combination, but adding the apple and tomato makes it a little different from what you might expect.

Serves
4

Cooking Time
35 Minutes

Release Method
Natural-release

1 teaspoon salt

freshly ground black pepper

½ teaspoon dried thyme

½ teaspoon dried oregano

¼ teaspoon dried basil

1 (2-pound) shoulder of pork, trimmed of excess fat and cut into 1½- to 2-inch chunks

1 to 2 tablespoons olive oil

1 onion, sliced

2 large carrots, peeled and cut into 3 large chunks each (or baby cut carrots)

2 cloves garlic, smashed

1 large tomato, cut into large chunks

1 bay leaf

½ small cabbage, cut into wedges (1-inch thick at widest point)

2 small apples, peeled and diced

1 (15-ounce) jar marinara sauce

¾ cup chicken stock

¼ cup chopped fresh parsley

1. Combine the salt, pepper, thyme, oregano and basil and toss the chunks of pork in this spice mixture.

2. Pre-heat the pressure cooker using the BROWN setting.

3. Add the oil and brown the pork in batches. Set the pork aside and add the onion, carrots and garlic to the cooker. Sauté until the onion starts to soften slightly – about 5 minutes. Add the tomato and bay leaf and return the browned pork to the cooker. Place a layer of cabbage wedges on top of the pork and scatter the diced apple over the top. Repeat with the remaining cabbage and diced apple. Combine the marinara sauce and the chicken stock and pour the mixture over the top of everything. Lock the lid in place.

4. Pressure cook on HIGH for 35 minutes.

5. Let the pressure drop NATURALLY and carefully remove the lid. Season the stew to taste with salt and pepper. Serve in a deep bowl over rice and sprinkle chopped fresh parsley on top.

Did You Know...?

Pork shoulder is also called pork butt, or Boston butt. That's not very intuitive in our modern day language, but the word "butt" actually derives from Old English meaning "an extremity" and usually the "widest part". On a pig, the widest part is actually the shoulder, not the rear end!

Asian Country-Style Pork Ribs

You can use two pounds of bone-in country style ribs here if you choose to, and they'll be super tasty, but you won't get as many servings out of the recipe as when you use boneless ribs, which take up less room. It's all about the tender meat in this recipe, so boneless ribs work really well.

Serves
4

Cooking Time
35 Minutes

Release Method
Natural-release

2½ pounds boneless country style ribs

salt and freshly ground black pepper

1 tablespoon Chinese 5-spice powder

2 tablespoons vegetable oil

½ cup sherry or Madeira wine

1 cup beef stock

½ cup blackberry preserves

1 clove garlic, minced

2 tablespoons fresh gingerroot, minced

½ cup hoisin sauce

1 scallion, chopped

1 tablespoon toasted sesame seeds

fresh cilantro leaves

1. Pre-heat the pressure cooker using the BROWN setting.

2. Season the ribs with salt, pepper and the 5-spice powder. Add the oil to the cooker and sear the ribs for 8 to 10 minutes. Remove the ribs from the cooker and set aside. Drain any excess grease from the cooker.

3. Add the sherry wine, beef stock, blackberry preserves, garlic, ginger and hoisin sauce and stir well. Return the ribs to the cooker, tossing to coat and lock the lid in place.

4. Pressure cook on HIGH for 35 minutes.

5. Let the pressure drop NATURALLY and carefully remove the lid. Serve the ribs garnished with the scallion, sesame seeds and cilantro.

Hoisin sauce is a thick sauce used in Chinese cooking, somewhat similar to BBQ sauce. You should be able to find jars of hoisin sauce it in the ethnic section of your grocery store.

Gumbo and Rice

There are several varieties of gumbo, a stew originating in Louisiana. Some have shellfish, while others do not. Gumbo is traditionally served over rice but in this version you cook the rice right into the gumbo, making an easy one-dish meal.

Serves
6

Cooking Time
5 Minutes

Release Method
Quick-release

1 tablespoon olive oil

1 pound Andouille pork sausage, cut into chunks

2 boneless skinless chicken breasts, cut into ½-inch pieces

1 onion, finely chopped

2 ribs celery, finely chopped

1 green bell pepper, finely chopped

3 cloves garlic, minced

¼ teaspoon cayenne pepper

½ teaspoon dried sage

½ teaspoon dried thyme

1 bay leaf

1½ cups long-grain rice

4 cups beef stock

1 (14 ounce) can chopped tomatoes

1 tablespoon tomato paste

5 ounces smoked ham, diced (about 1 cup)

2 teaspoons Worcestershire sauce

1 teaspoon salt

4 scallions, sliced

1. Pre-heat the pressure cooker using the BROWN setting.

2. Add the olive oil and brown the Andouille sausage and chicken pieces in batches. Remove the browned meats to a plate and set aside. Add the onion, celery, green pepper and garlic to the cooker and continue to cook for a few minutes. Stir in the spices and rice and cook for a minute or so, stirring to coat the rice with the oil.

3. Add the stock, tomatoes, tomato paste, ham, Worcestershire sauce and salt. Return the browned sausage and chicken to the cooker and lock the lid in place.

4. Pressure cook on HIGH for 5 minutes.

5. Reduce the pressure with the QUICK-RELEASE method and carefully remove the lid. Stir everything together and scatter the scallions over top before serving.

It's easy to add shellfish to this dish. After you release the pressure, simply nestle the shrimp into the dish and return the lid to the cooker for 3 to 5 minutes, or until the shrimp turn pink.

Braised Pork Shoulder with Sauerkraut

Pork, sauerkraut and apple all play the lead roles in this recipe that would please any hungry eater, whether you serve it on a plate or on a kaiser roll.

Serves
4 to 6

Cooking Time
40 Minutes

Release Method
Natural-release

1 (3-pound) shoulder of pork, trimmed of excess fat

salt and freshly ground black pepper

2 tablespoons olive oil

¼ pound bacon, diced

½ large white onion, chopped (about 1 cup)

1 large carrot, chopped

2 ribs celery, chopped

3 cloves garlic, smashed

3 sprigs fresh thyme

1 cup white wine

16 ounces good-quality sauerkraut

2 cups beef stock

1 cup applesauce

1 apple, cored and rough chopped

2 teaspoons fennel seed

2 teaspoons dried oregano

1. Pre-heat the pressure cooker using the BROWN setting.

2. Cut the pork to fit into the pressure cooker if necessary. Season the pork with salt and freshly ground black pepper. Add the oil to the cooker and sear the pork on all sides for 8 to 10 minutes, until deep brown. Remove the pork from the cooker and set aside. Drain the oil from the cooker.

3. Add the bacon to the cooker and cook for 5 minutes, stirring occasionally. Add the onion, carrot, celery, garlic and thyme, and cook for another 6 to 8 minutes. Pour in the wine, scraping up any brown bits on the bottom. Add the sauerkraut and cook for 5 minutes, stirring occasionally. Add the stock and all the remaining ingredients. Return the pork to the cooker and lock the lid in place.

4. Pressure cook on HIGH for 40 minutes.

5. Let the pressure drop NATURALLY and carefully remove the lid. Remove the pork to a plate to rest for at least five minutes. In the meantime, return the cooker to the BROWN setting and let the liquid reduce a little to concentrate the flavors. Season the sauerkraut to taste with salt and freshly ground black pepper. Serve the pork in large chunks along with some of the sauerkraut and vegetables.

Apple Stuffed Pork Chops

Cooking stuffed foods in the pressure cooker can be a challenge because the stuffing seems to always escape. With this recipe, you'll cut the slit in the end of the pork chop so that you can stand it upright when it cooks and the stuffing will remain inside.

Serves
4

Cooking Time
4 Minutes

Release Method
Natural-release

¼ cup butter

½ onion, chopped

2 ribs celery, diced

½ cup chicken stock

1 cup apple, peeled and diced
(Roma or Gala are good choices)

2 cups herbed seasoned stuffing cubes

4 thick boneless center-cut pork chops

salt and freshly ground black pepper

1 teaspoon dried thyme

1 tablepoon olive oil

1 cup chicken stock

½ cup white wine

1. Pre-heat the pressure cooker using the BROWN setting.

2. Add the butter to the cooker and cook the onion and celery for a few minutes, until the vegetables start to soften. Add half a cup of the chicken stock and apples to the cooker, along with the stuffing mix and stir to combine. Transfer this mixture to a bowl and wipe out the inside of cooker.

3. While the stuffing is cooling, prepare the pork chops. Lay the chops flat on a cutting board and press down on the pork chop with the palm of your hand. Use a sharp thin knife to cut a deep slit into the top of the pork chop (one of the short sides of the chop) making a "pocket" in the chop, but not cutting through the sides or bottom of the chop. When the stuffing has cooled, push the stuffing into the pocket in the pork chop, pushing it down with your fingers as far into the pocket as you can.

4. Pre-heat the pressure cooker using the BROWN setting again. Season the outside of the pork chops with salt, pepper and thyme. Add the olive to pressure cooker and carefully brown the outside of the pork chops on both sides. Handle the chops carefully so that the stuffing doesn't get squeezed out of the chop.

5. Place a rack in the pressure cooker and place the pork chops on top of the rack, with the pocket facing up. The chops should lean on each other to stay upright. Pour the remaining chicken stock and white wine into the cooker.

6. Pressure cook on HIGH for 4 minutes.

7. Let the pressure drop NATURALLY and carefully remove the lid. Remove the stuffed pork chops to a resting plate for a few minutes before serving.

If you'd like to make a sauce for the chops, mix 2 tablespoons of soft butter with 2 tablespoons of flour to make a paste. Remove any bits of stuffing from the cooker with a slotted spoon and stir the butter mixture into the sauce. Return the cooker to the BROWN setting and bring everything to a simmer to thicken. Add a little fresh thyme and season with salt and pepper.

Asian Meatballs

These meatballs stay moist because of the mushrooms inside, which give off liquid as they cook. You can use any dipping sauce you like, but Thai sweet chili sauce is easy and delicious.

Serves
18 Meatballs

Cooking Time
5 Minutes

Release Method
Natural-release

1 large shallot, finely chopped

2 scallions, very finely chopped

2 cloves garlic, minced

1 tablespoon grated fresh gingerroot

2 teaspoons fresh thyme, finely chopped

1½ cups brown or shiitake mushrooms, very finely chopped (a food processor works well here)

2 tablespoons soy sauce

freshly ground black pepper

1 pound ground pork

½ pound ground beef

3 egg yolks

1 tablespoon vegetable oil

2 cups chicken stock

1 cup Thai sweet chili sauce (for dipping)

1. Combine the shallot, scallions, garlic, ginger, thyme, mushrooms, soy sauce, black pepper, ground pork and beef, and egg yolks in a bowl and gently mix the ingredients together. Gently shape the mixture into golf ball-sized balls.

2. Pre-heat the pressure cooker using the BROWN setting.

3. Add some of the oil to the cooker and brown the meatballs in batches, using more oil as necessary. Remove the browned meatballs to a plate and set aside. Add the chicken stock to the pressure cooker and place either a rack or a steamer basket inside. Transfer the meatballs to the rack or steamer basket in the pressure cooker and lock the lid in place.

4. Cook on HIGH pressure for 5 minutes.

5. Let the pressure drop NATURALLY and carefully remove the lid.

6. Transfer the meatballs to a serving dish and serve with the sweet chili sauce for dipping.

Use a small ice cream scoop to quickly and uniformly shape the meatballs. Chilling the meatballs in the freezer for 15 minutes before browning helps them keep their round shape.

Fish
and
Seafood

Paella

Grouper with Orange Couscous

Salmon with Lemon Herbed Rice

Thai Coconut Mussels

Lime Shrimp and Spicy Tomato Grits

Cod with Tomatoes, Potatoes and Spinach

Provençal Fish Stew with Fennel and Potatoes

Paella

There are generally three different types of Paella: those with just seafood, those with just meat, and mixed paellas - those with both meat and seafood. This is a mixed paella, which means there's something for everyone included!

Serves
4 to 6

Cooking Time
4 Minutes

Release Method
Quick-release

1 tablespoon olive oil

1 link Chorizo sausage, sliced

2 boneless skinless chicken breasts, cut into ½-inch pieces

1 onion, finely chopped

1 red bell pepper, finely chopped

3 cloves garlic, minced

1 cup short-grain rice

pinch saffron threads

½ teaspoon Spanish paprika

½ teaspoon dried oregano

2 cups chicken stock

1 (14-ounce) can diced tomatoes

8 mussels, scrubbed and de-bearded

8 clams, scrubbed

8 large raw shrimp, peeled and de-veined

salt and freshly ground black pepper

¼ cup chopped fresh parsley

5 scallions, sliced

1. Pre-heat the pressure cooker using the BROWN setting.

2. Add the olive oil and brown the sausage and chicken in batches. Remove the browned meats to a plate and set aside. Add the onion, red pepper and garlic to the cooker and continue to cook for a few minutes. Add the rice and spices, crumbling the saffron between your fingers as you add it. Stir to coat the rice with the oil and return the browned sausage and chicken to the cooker. Stir in the stock and tomatoes, drop the mussels and clams on top and lock the lid in place.

3. Pressure cook on HIGH for 4 minutes.

4. Reduce the pressure with the QUICK-RELEASE method and carefully remove the lid.

5. Add the shrimp to the cooker, tucking them into the rice and return the lid to the cooker for 3 to 5 minutes or until all the shrimp has cooked and turned bright pink. Stir everything together, adding the parsley and seasoning to taste with salt and pepper. Scatter the scallions over top before serving.

Grouper with Orange Couscous

Citrus and seafood go so well together. In this recipe, the grouper cooks in orange juice and is then served on a bed of couscous flavored with the same orange juice, along with currants, almonds and olive oil.

Serves
4

Cooking Time
3 Minutes

Release Method
Quick-release

1 tablespoon olive oil

½ onion, finely chopped

1 rib celery, finely chopped

1 small carrot, finely chopped

¾ cup orange juice

½ cup chicken stock

1 bay leaf

4 (5-ounce) fillets grouper (or red snapper fillets)

salt and freshly ground black pepper

1 cup couscous

¼ cup dried currants

¼ cup slivered almonds

½ orange, zest and juice

2 tablespoons extra virgin olive oil

1. Pre-heat the pressure cooker using the BROWN setting.

2. Add the oil and sauté the onion, celery and carrot for five minutes, until the onion starts to soften. Pour in ¾ cup orange juice and chicken stock, and add the bay leaf. Season the fish fillets well with salt and freshly ground black pepper and place them into the cooker, skin side down. Lock the lid in place.

3. Pressure cook on HIGH for 3 minutes.

4. Release the pressure using the QUICK-RELEASE method and carefully remove the lid. Gently remove the fish fillets to a plate to rest.

5. Stir the couscous and currants into the broth and cover with the lid for 5 minutes. Fluff the couscous and add the almonds, orange zest and juice and olive oil. Season to taste with salt and freshly ground black pepper, and serve the fish and couscous with a tossed salad or green vegetable.

Salmon with Lemon Herbed Rice

Make sure you're hungry for dinner before you start cooking because this dish is made so quickly, you'll be hard pressed to lay the table before it's done! There is no prep work involved and you have just 5 minutes while the fish and rice cook to chop the herbs that go in at the end.

Serves
4

Cooking Time
5 Minutes

Release Method
Quick-release

1 tablespoon butter

1 cup long-grain rice, rinsed

1½ cups water (or chicken stock)

1 teaspoon salt

freshly ground black pepper

4 (5-ounce) fillets of salmon

2 tablespoons chopped fresh chives

2 tablespoons chopped fresh parsley

lemon juice, to taste

1. Add the butter, rice, water and salt to the pressure cooker. Season the salmon with salt and pepper and place the fillets on top of the rice gently. Lock the lid in place.

2. Pressure cook on HIGH for 5 minutes.

3. Reduce the pressure with QUICK-RELEASE method and carefully remove the lid. Transfer the salmon to a side plate to rest. Fluff the rice with the herbs and season with lemon juice and more salt to taste.

4. Serve the salmon and rice along with a side vegetable or salad.

Thai Coconut Mussels

The general rule of thumb is one pound of mussels per person as an entrée, but as a starter course, this recipe will feed four people. Don't forget to put a bowl out for the shells when you serve this regarless of what course it is!

Serves
2

Cooking Time
4 Minutes

Release Method
Quick-release

2 pounds mussels

1 tablespoon coconut or vegetable oil

2 to 3 shallots (or 1 small onion), sliced

1 clove garlic, sliced

1 inch of fresh gingerroot, peeled and thinly sliced

1 Thai red chili pepper, sliced
(or if you do not want any spice, use a red bell pepper)

½ cup dry white wine

1 (15-ounce) can unsweetened coconut milk

zest and juice of one lime

¼ cup chopped fresh basil

freshly ground black pepper

1. Clean the mussels by scrubbing them with a brush under running water. Pull off the beard (the whiskery hairs protruding from the shell). Discard any mussels that are open, broken or don't close their shells when tapped.

2. Pre-heat the pressure cooker using the BROWN setting.

3. Add the oil and sauté the shallot, garlic, ginger and red chili pepper for 2 to 3 minutes. Add the wine and coconut milk and stir. Add all the mussels and lock the lid in place.

4. Pressure cook on HIGH for 4 minutes.

5. Release the pressure using the QUICK-RELEASE method and carefully remove the lid. Transfer the mussels to a serving dish, discarding any mussels that did not open (do not force them open). Sprinkle the lime zest and basil on top and squeeze the lime over everything.

Did You Know...?

Lite Coconut milk is really just watered down regular coconut milk. The trouble is that the flavor is really watered down too, so I recommend using the real deal!

Lime Shrimp and Spicy Tomato Grits

Shrimp and grits are often in each other's company, but here the shrimp actually cook in the grits, rather than sitting on top at the end. This is a great marinade for grilled shrimp too.

Serves
4

Cooking Time
10 Minutes

Release Method
Natural-release

1 pound large shrimp, peeled, deveined and tails removed (about 16 to 20)

¼ cup olive oil

1 clove garlic, sliced

1 tablespoon crushed red pepper flakes

1 tablespoon finely chopped lime zest (about 2 limes)

¼ cup fresh lime juice (about 1½ limes)

2 tablespoons butter

1 Jalapeño pepper, de-seeded and minced

⅛ teaspoon ground cayenne pepper

2 tablespoons tomato paste

4 cups water

1 teaspoon salt

1 cup coarse corn grits
(not the instant variety)

2 tomatoes, chopped

chopped fresh chives

1. Start by marinating the shrimp. Combine the olive oil, garlic, crushed red pepper flakes, lime zest and juice in a bowl and toss in shrimp. Set the shrimp aside while you prepare the grits.

2. Pre-heat the pressure cooker using the BROWN setting. Add the butter and Jalapeño pepper and sauté for a couple of minutes. Add the cayenne pepper and tomato paste and stir, cooking for another minute or two. Add the water and salt and bring the mixture to a boil. Whisk the grits into the water, whisking for a full minute so that the grits have a moment to become suspended in the water and not drop to the bottom of the pot. Lock the lid in place.

3. Pressure cook on HIGH for 10 minutes.

4. Let the pressure drop NATURALLY and carefully remove the lid. Give the grits a good stir – they will probably have settled somewhat on the bottom of the cooker. Once you've stirred the grits, immediately remove the shrimp from the marinade with a slotted spoon and stir them into the grits along with the fresh tomatoes. Return the lid to the cooker for 5 minutes. There will be enough residual heat to cook the shrimp through. Season to taste with salt and serve with fresh chives on top.

When you are serving shrimp in a dish, think about your guests. When shrimp are stirred right into a dish, remove the tail before you add them to the pot so that your guests don't have embarrassing moments trying to remove the tail themselves.

Cod with Tomatoes, Potatoes and Spinach

This is a nice, light and delicious dinner made in under 5 minutes. Any fish fillets that are at least one inch thick will work nicely in this recipe. Serve in a shallow bowl with some crusty bread to mop up the delicious broth.

Serves
4

Cooking Time
5 Minutes

Release Method
Quick-release

2 cups unsalted chicken stock (if you're using salted stock, reduce the salt below)

2 cloves garlic, smashed

2 cups halved cherry tomatoes (about 10 ounces)

2 cups diced yellow potato (½-inch dice) (about 10 ounces)

1 teaspoon salt

freshly ground black pepper

4 (5- to 6-ounce) fillets of cod

5 ounces baby spinach leaves (about 5 cups, packed)

lemon juice, to taste

1. Add the stock, garlic, tomatoes, potatoes, salt and pepper to the pressure cooker. Season the fillets of cod with salt and pepper and place into the broth. Lock the lid in place.

2. Pressure cook on HIGH for 5 minutes.

3. Reduce the pressure with QUICK-RELEASE method and carefully remove the lid. Transfer the cod to a side plate to rest. Stir the spinach into the stock and vegetables and let it wilt for a minute or two while the fish rests. Season the broth with salt and pepper and a squeeze of lemon juice to taste.

4. Serve the cod, vegetables and broth in a shallow bowl with a piece of crusty bread to soak up the remaining liquid.

Provençal Fish Stew with Fennel and Potatoes

If you like seafood, you'll love this seafood stew. It's not only delicious, but pretty too with all the different types of seafood included. There aren't too many year-round stews, but this is one of them.

Serves
4

Cooking Time
4 Minutes

Release Method
Quick-release

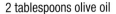

2 tablespoons olive oil

1 onion, finely chopped

1 clove garlic, peeled and smashed

1 teaspoon dried thyme

1 tablespoon tomato paste

2 Yukon Gold potatoes, diced (1-inch)

1 bulb fennel, diced (1-inch)

½ cup dry white wine

1 (28-ounce) can tomatoes, chopped

2 cups seafood stock (or chicken stock if you can't find seafood stock)

1 teaspoon saffron threads (optional)

8 ounces salmon, cut into 1-inch chunks

8 ounces grouper or red snapper, cut into 1-inch chunks

salt and freshly ground black pepper

12 to 16 mussels

8 medium shrimp, peeled, deveined and tails removed.

3 tablespoons anise-flavored liquor (Pernod, Pastis) (optional)

zest of one orange

¼ cup chopped fresh parsley

1. Pre-heat the pressure cooker using the BROWN setting.

2. Add the olive oil and sauté the onion and garlic until the onion starts to become tender – about 5 minutes. Add the thyme and tomato paste, stir and cook for a minute or two. Add the potatoes, fennel, white wine, tomatoes, stock, saffron (if using) and fish. Stir and season with salt and pepper. Toss the mussels in on top of the stew and lock the lid in place.

3. Cook on HIGH pressure for 4 minutes.

4. Release the pressure using the QUICK-RELEASE method and carefully remove the lid. Immediately add the shrimp to the stew and return the lid to the cooker for three to four minutes. There will be enough residual heat to cook the shrimp, which will change color to bright pink.

5. Stir in the anise-flavored liquor (if using), orange zest and parsley. Remove and discard any mussels whose shells did not open, and serve the stew with a nice chunk of crusty bread to soak up the juices.

If you can't find Pernod or Pastis for this recipe, try dry vermouth instead. You might be tempted to try to use Sambuca (another anise or licorice flavored liqueur), but that is a sugar-based liqueur that wouldn't work well with this savory stew.

Vegetarian Main Dishes

Great Northern Beans with Cauliflower, Fennel and Feta

Aloo Gobi - Potato and Cauliflower Curry

Risotto with Shiitake Mushrooms, Butternut Squash & Peas

Broccoli Rice Casserole

Chickpea, Cabbage and Tomato Stew

Miso Brown Rice Bowl w/ Tofu and Edamame

Red Lentil Bolognese

Warm Cauliflower and Three Bean Salad

Spaghetti Squash with Leek and Olive Marinara

Great Northern Beans with Cauliflower, Fennel and Feta

This is a room temperature salad that looks so elegant and is so satisfying. It's a tasty vegetarian entrée but can also be served as a side dish to another main meal.

Serves
4

Cooking Time
10 + 2 Minutes

Release Method
Combo

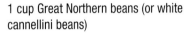

1 cup Great Northern beans (or white cannellini beans)

1 small head cauliflower, broken into florets (about 2 cups)

4 sprigs fresh thyme

salt and freshly ground black pepper

1½ cups water

1 small bulb fennel, thinly sliced

juice of ½ lemon

3 tablespoons extra virgin olive oil

2 tablespoons chopped fresh chives

2 tablespoons chopped fresh parsley

2 tablespoons chopped fresh basil

1½ cups crumbled feta cheese

1. Place the beans in the pressure cooker and cover with at least 1-inch of water. Lock the lid in place.

2. Pressure cook on HIGH For 10 minutes.

3. Let the pressure drop NATURALLY and carefully remove the lid. Strain the beans and return them to the hot cooker. Add the cauliflower florets and thyme sprigs. Season with salt and freshly ground black pepper. Add the water and lock the lid in place.

4. Pressure cook on HIGH for 2 minutes.

5. Release the pressure using the QUICK-RELEASE method and carefully remove the lid. Transfer the beans and cauliflower to a large bowl with a slotted spoon. Add the fennel to the bowl and toss with the lemon juice, olive oil and fresh herbs. When well mixed, toss one more time gently with the feta cheese and season to taste with salt and pepper.

Did You Know...?

The feta cheese plays a critical role in this dish, really seasoning the dish, so look for the best feta you can find. A good feta cheese should be made of only sheep's milk, come from Greece, be packed in brine, have a white color (not cream) and a few tiny holes on the surface. Of course, the best way to pick a good feta is to taste it, if you have that chance.

Aloo Gobi
(Potato and Cauliflower Curry)

The potatoes in this gorgeous vegetable curry break down in the pressure cooker, thickening the sauce a little. There's not much sauce at the end – just enough to coat the vegetables. So, if the sauce is what you're all about, increase the vegetable stock by half a cup.

Serves
2 to 4

Cooking Time
5 Minutes

Release Method
Quick-release

1 tablespoon olive oil

1 tablespoon butter

1 onion, chopped

1 clove garlic, minced

2 teaspoons grated fresh ginger root

1 tablespoon curry powder

1 teaspoon brown mustard seeds

4 Yukon Gold potatoes, scrubbed and cut into chunks (1-inch chunks)

1 head cauliflower, cut or broken into florets

1 red chili pepper, sliced

1 cup vegetable stock

1 teaspoon salt

2 tablespoons fresh cilantro leaves (or parsley)

1. Pre-heat the pressure cooker using the BROWN setting. Add the olive oil and butter, and sauté the onion until it starts to get tender – about 5 minutes. Add the garlic, ginger and spices and continue to cook, stirring for another 2 minutes. Add the potatoes, cauliflower and chili pepper and do your best to stir everything together. (You can do this more easily if you transfer everything to a big bowl, toss and then return it to the cooker.) Pour in the vegetable stock, season with salt, and lock the lid in place.

2. Pressure cook on HIGH for 5 minutes.

3. Release the pressure using the QUICK-RELEASE method and carefully remove the lid. Toss the vegetables together into a serving bowl, pouring the cooking liquid over the top. Garnish with leaves of fresh cilantro.

 Substitution

The brown mustard seeds are not only a flavoring component, but also a visual garnish for this dish. But, if you can't find brown mustard seeds, you can substitute yellow mustard seeds.

Risotto with Shiitake Mushrooms, Butternut Squash and Peas

Long gone are the days when making risotto required standing over a stovetop stirring constantly for twenty to thirty minutes. Almost miraculously, a pressure cooker can deliver a risotto in just seven minutes, no stirring required. Using this recipe as a base, you can make any flavored risotto you like.

Serves
6

Cooking Time
7 Minutes

Release Method
Quick-release

1 tablespoon olive oil

1 small onion, finely chopped

3 sprigs fresh thyme

1½ cups ½-inch diced butternut squash

2 cups thinly sliced shiitake mushrooms, stems removed (about 5 ounces)

1½ cups Arborio rice

½ cup white wine

1 cup vegetable stock

2½ cups water

2 teaspoons salt

freshly ground black pepper

½ cup frozen peas, thawed

½ cup grated Parmigiano-Reggiano cheese

1. Pre-heat the pressure cooker using the BROWN setting.

2. Add the oil and cook the onion for a few minutes. Add the thyme, butternut squash and mushrooms and cook for another few minutes. Add the rice, wine, vegetable stock, water, salt and freshly ground black pepper, give everything one good stir and lock the lid in place.

3. Pressure cook on HIGH for 7 minutes.

4. Release the pressure using the QUICK-RELEASE method and carefully remove the lid. Remove the thyme sprigs, stir in the peas and close the lid for 2 minutes to let them warm through. Stir in the cheese and season to taste with salt and freshly ground black pepper.

You can use either short-grained Arborio or medium-grained Carnaroli rice for risotto. Carnaroli rice is not as common as Arborio. It has a firmer texture, but still produces a creamy risotto because it has a high starch content.

Broccoli Rice Casserole

You can use fresh OR frozen broccoli florets for this recipe, which makes it a perfect pantry dinner – all the ingredients can be stored in your pantry or freezer, so you'll always be able to make this dish.

Serves
2 to 4

Cooking Time
5 Minutes

Release Method
Quick-release

1 tablespoon vegetable oil

½ onion, finely chopped

pinch crushed red pepper flakes

1 teaspoon dried thyme

1 cup basmati rice

1 cup water

1 (10-ounce) can cream of mushroom soup

2 stalks broccoli, broken into medium sized florets (or 3 cups frozen broccoli florets)

salt, to taste

2 cups grated Cheddar cheese

1. Pre-heat the pressure cooker using the BROWN setting.

2. Add the oil and sauté the onion, red pepper flakes and thyme until the onion starts to soften – about 5 minutes. Add the rice and stir to coat the rice with the oil. Combine the water and mushroom soup, pour the mixture into the cooker and give everything a good stir. Finally, add the broccoli florets, scattering them across the top of the rice. Season with salt and lock the lid in place.

3. Pressure cook on HIGH for 5 minutes.

4. Release the pressure using the QUICK-RELEASE method and carefully remove the lid. Scatter the grated Cheddar cheese on top and return the lid to the cooker for 10 minutes. The rice will continue to steam, the cheese will melt and the casserole will cool to an edible temperature.

Did You Know...?

You can also add the broccoli stems to this recipe. Just make sure you dice the stalks into ½-inch dice.

Chickpea, Cabbage and Tomato Stew

This stew is reminiscent of a Hungarian goulash or paprikash dish. The chickpeas provide a good source of protein and the sour cream at the end gives it a creamy saucy finish.

Serves
4

Cooking Time
5 + 20 Minutes

Release Method
Combo

1 cup dried chickpeas

2 tablespoons vegetable or olive oil

1 onion, thinly sliced

1 carrot, thinly sliced on the bias

2 cloves garlic, minced

¼ teaspoon crushed red pepper flakes

2 tablespoons sweet Hungarian paprika

1 teaspoon dried thyme

1 teaspoon salt

freshly ground black pepper

4 cups sliced cabbage, ½-inch thick slices (about ¼ large cabbage)

1 (28-ounce) can tomatoes, chopped

2 tablespoons tomato paste

1 cup vegetable stock or water

½ cup sour cream

¼ cup chopped fresh parsley

1. Place the chickpeas in the pressure cooker and cover with at least 1-inch of water. Lock the lid in place. Pressure cook on HIGH For 5 minutes. Let the pressure drop NATURALLY and carefully remove the lid. Strain the chickpeas and set them aside.

2. Pre-heat the pressure cooker using the BROWN setting.

3. Add the oil and sauté the onion and carrot for a few minutes, until the onion starts to soften. Add the garlic and spices and cook for another minute or two. Stir in the cabbage, tomatoes, tomato paste and stock, and return the chickpeas to the cooker. Lock the lid in place.

4. Pressure cook for 20 minutes.

5. Release the pressure using the QUICK-RELEASE method and carefully remove the lid. Let the broth cool a little and then season to taste with salt and freshly ground black pepper. Stir in the sour cream and parsley, and serve with some crusty bread.

Miso Brown Rice Bowl with Tofu and Edamame

There are so many health benefits to this meal that I don't have room to list them here. But, health benefits are not what make us want to eat dinner. It's the sweet and salty miso sauce flavor that really makes this a rice bowl you'll want to come back to again and again. I have to give recipe credit here to my friend, Lynn who is an excellent cook and brought great flavors to the table with this recipe.

Serves
6 to 8

Cooking Time
20 Minutes

Release Method
Natural-release

¼ cup light miso paste

¼ cup soy sauce

2 tablespoons minced fresh ginger (peeled)

2 cloves garlic, minced

⅛ teaspoon ground cayenne

4 teaspoons rice vinegar

¼ cup mirin (Japanese sweet rice wine)

2 tablespoons honey

1 tablespoon toasted sesame seeds

3 scallions, thinly sliced (white and light green parts only)

1 pound extra firm tofu, drained and cut into small cubes

1½ cups brown rice

1 red bell pepper, finely chopped

1 carrot, peeled and grated

1½ cups vegetable broth

1 (8-ounce) bag frozen edamame (soy beans), defrosted

1. To make the miso sauce, mix together the first ten ingredients in a bowl and stir well.

2. In a separate bowl, toss the tofu with ¼ cup of the miso sauce. Set aside.

3. Place the brown rice, red pepper, carrot, vegetable broth and ¼ cup of the miso sauce into the pressure cooker. Lock the lid in place.

4. Pressure cook on HIGH for 20 minutes.

5. Let the pressure drop NATURALLY and carefully remove the lid.

6. Fold the tofu and edamame into the rice. Return the lid to the cooker and let the mixture sit for a minute or two to warm the tofu and edamame. Serve with the remaining sauce at the table.

Miso is a Japanese seasoning paste made from fermented soybeans. While that might not sound very appetizing, it's a delicious salty seasoning with health benefits to boot! Miso is a complete protein that aids in digestion, boosts the immune system and can lower bad cholesterol. You will find miso in a tub, refrigerated, often near the produce section with other refrigerated dressings.

If you can't find mirin – a sweet Japanese cooking wine – then you can substitute dry sherry, sweet marsala or white wine with a good pinch of sugar.

Red Lentil Bolognese

This recipe is for the pasta lover who wants to feed a crowd. Cook the pasta separately for this dish, and leave the room in the pressure cooker for a lot of sauce. Red lentils are used here because, even though they turn yellow as they cook, the final appearance is nicer than when you use green or brown lentils.

Serves
8 to 10

Cooking Time
6 Minutes

Release Method
Combo

1 to 2 tablespoons olive oil

1 onion, finely chopped

2 carrots, very finely chopped

2 ribs of celery, finely chopped

2 cloves garlic, minced

1½ cups red lentils

1 teaspoon dried oregano

1 teaspoon dried thyme

1 bay leaf

2 teaspoons salt

freshly ground black pepper

1 (28 ounce) can tomatoes, chopped

2 tablespoons tomato paste

2 cups vegetable stock

¼ cup chopped fresh parsley

1. Pre-heat the pressure cooker using the BROWN setting.

2. Add the oil to the cooker and cook the onion, carrots, and celery for a few minutes, until the vegetables start to soften. Add the garlic and lentils and cook for another minute or two. Add the oregano, thyme, bay leaf, salt and pepper, tomatoes, tomato paste and vegetable stock, stir and lock the lid in place.

3. Pressure cook on HIGH for 6 minutes.

4. Let the pressure drop NATURALLY for 5 minutes. Then, release any residual pressure using the QUICK-RELEASE method and carefully remove the lid. Stir in the parsley and season to taste with salt and freshly ground black pepper.

5. Serve over cooked spaghetti with some grated Parmigiano-Reggiano cheese.

The lentils will continue to absorb moisture as they sit, so be sure to thin the sauce to the desired consistency with water or vegetable stock if you're serving this the next day. A little reserved pasta water after you cook your spaghetti is perfect for that.

Warm Cauliflower and Three Bean Salad

The beauty of this warm salad is being able to cook the beans from their dried form in just 25 minutes! Then, just another quick minute for the cauliflower and green beans and toss it all together with a zippy vinaigrette. This is also tasty cold or room temperature, so it makes a great dish to take somewhere.

VEG ETARIAN

Serves
8 to 10

Cooking Time
25 + 1 Minutes

Release Method
Combo

½ cup dried white cannellini beans

½ cup dried kidney beans

1 teaspoon salt

1 tablespoon sugar

2 tablespoons cider vinegar

¼ cup extra virgin olive oil

1 tablespoon chopped fresh chives

¼ cup chopped sun-dried tomatoes

juice of ½ lemon

freshly ground black pepper

½ head cauliflower, cut into small florets

2 cups trimmed green beans, cut into 2-inch pieces

½ cup chopped walnuts, toasted

¼ cup parsley, roughly chopped

1. Place the two different beans in the pressure cooker together and cover with an inch of water.

2. Pressure cook on HIGH for 25 minutes, and then let the pressure drop NATURALLY. Carefully remove the lid, drain the beans and set aside.

3. While the beans are cooking, make the dressing by whisking together the salt, sugar, vinegar, olive oil, chives, sun-dried tomatoes, lemon juice and freshly ground black pepper. Set aside.

4. Place the cauliflower and green beans into the cooker along with 1 cup of water. Pressure cook on HIGH for 1 minute. Release the pressure using the QUICK-RELEASE method and carefully remove the lid. Drain the vegetables and set aside.

5. Combine the drained cannellini and kidney beans with the warm cauliflower and green beans, walnuts and parsley and toss with the dressing.

Spaghetti Squash with Leek and Olive Marinara

Few meals leave me feeling as fresh and healthy as a bowl of spaghetti squash with marinara sauce. Cooking the squash in the pressure cooker saves so much time and is easy and tidy. While the squash cools, there's just enough time to make a delicious marinara to go over the top. Remember to top it all with true Parmigiano-Reggiano cheese – there is no substitute!

Serves
4 to 6

Cooking Time
15 + 5 Minutes

Release Method
Quick-release

1 spaghetti squash, halved and seeds removed

salt and freshly ground black pepper

2 tablespoons olive oil

2 leeks, cleaned and sliced 1-inch thick (about 3 cups)

3 cloves garlic, finely chopped

¼ teaspoon crushed red pepper flakes

1 teaspoon dried oregano

¾ cup pitted black olives, halved

1 (28-ounce) can tomatoes, chopped

1 (28-ounce) can tomatoes, crushed

2 tablespoons tomato paste

½ cup water

½ cup grated Parmigiano-Reggiano cheese

¼ cup chopped fresh parsley

1. Cut the spaghetti squash halves to fit your pressure cooker insert. Season the cut side of the spaghetti squash with salt and pepper. Place the spaghetti squash, cut side down on a rack in the pressure cooker. (It's alright if they are stacked on top of each other or lop-sided.) Add 2 cups of water to the cooker and lock the lid in place.

2. Pressure cook on HIGH for 15 minutes (depending on the size of the spaghetti squash).

3. Release the pressure using the QUICK-RELEASE method and carefully remove the lid. Remove the spaghetti squash halves from the cooker using tongs and set aside to cool.

4. While the spaghetti squash cools, make the marinara. Empty and clean the pressure cooker insert. Pre-heat the pressure cooker using the BROWN setting. Add the olive oil and sauté the leeks until they start to turn brown on the edges – about 4 minutes. Add the garlic, crushed red pepper flakes, oregano and olives and cook for another minute or two. Add the tomatoes, tomato paste and water, season with salt and lock the lid in place.

5. Pressure cook on HIGH for 5 minutes.

6. Release the pressure using the QUICK-RELEASE method and carefully remove the lid. When the spaghetti squash is cool enough to handle, scrape the squash with a fork, pulling the strands of squash away from the skin. Season the strands of squash with salt and freshly ground black pepper to taste and then top with the marinara. Sprinkle the Parmigiano-Reggiano cheese and parsley on top just before serving.

 *Shortcut*

If you're really in a hurry, you can start the marinara sauce in a sauté pan on the stovetop while the spaghetti squash is cooking in the pressure cooker. Once all the ingredients are in the pan, remove the pan from the heat. As soon as the spaghetti squash has finished cooking, add the sauce ingredients to the pressure cooker, lock the lid in place and cook. In the quick five minutes it takes for the spaghetti squash to cool, the sauce will be done.

Grains and Beans

Farro Salad with Hazelnuts, Arugula and Grapes

Safron Rice with Chickpeas

White Beans with Pancetta and Kale

Ham and Cheddar Grits

Quinoa Rice with Almonds

Rice and Vegetable Pilaf

Brown Rice Salad with Artichoke Hearts, Avocado and Pinenuts

Baked Beans

Farro Salad
with Hazelnuts, Arugula and Grapes

Farro was the primary grain in Ancient Rome and some consider it to be the "original wheat species". It's easy to cook, has a delicious nutty flavor, is high in fiber and is a good source of protein and iron. What's better than easy, healthy AND delicious?

Serves
4

Cooking Time
18 Minutes

Release Method
Quick-release

1 cup farro

3 cups water

pinch of salt

2 cups arugula

½ cup toasted hazelnuts

1 cup seedless red grapes, halved

2 teaspoons orange zest

¼ cup fresh parsley leaves, rough chopped

¼ cup fresh mint leaves, rough chopped

2 teaspoons white balsamic vinegar

2 tablespoons extra virgin olive oil

salt and freshly ground black pepper, to taste

1. Place the farro and water in the pressure cooker, along with a good pinch of salt and lock the lid in place.

2. Pressure cook on HIGH for 18 minutes.

3. While the farro is cooking, prepare the remaining ingredients by combining the arugula, hazelnuts, grapes, orange zest and herbs in a large bowl. In a separate small bowl, whisk the white balsamic vinegar, extra virgin olive oil, salt and freshly ground black pepper together and set aside.

4. Release the pressure using the QUICK-RELEASE method and carefully remove the lid. Strain the farro, discarding any excess liquid, and spread it out onto a cookie sheet to let it cool for about 10 minutes. Then, add the farro to the bowl with the remaining ingredients and toss everything together with the vinaigrette. Serve at room temperature.

Dress It Up

This salad is also delicious with fresh pomegranate. The tidiest way to get pomegranate seeds (called arils) out of the pomegranate is to cut the pomegranate in quarters and then submerge each piece in a bowl of water while you pick out the seeds with your fingers. The bitter white pith will rise to the surface of the water. Scoop that up with your hands and discard. Strain off the water and you'll be left with just the seeds...or arils. Alternately, you can bang the back of the pomegranate half with a wooden spoon over a bowl and the arils will drop out of the pomegranate into the bowl.

Saffron Rice with Chickpeas

I love chickpeas (also called Garbanzo beans)! I also love mixing beans and rice together. Throw some saffron in the mix, making them a pretty yellow color and I'm a happy cook!

Serves
4

Cooking Time
5 + 6 Minutes

Release Method
Combo

¾ cup dried chickpeas

1 tablespoon vegetable oil

1 tablespoon butter

½ onion, finely chopped

2 cloves garlic, sliced

1 teaspoon saffron threads

1 cup basmati rice

1¾ cups water

1½ teaspoons salt

freshly ground black pepper

¼ cup chopped fresh cilantro or parsley

water

1. Place the chickpeas in the pressure cooker and cover with an inch of water. Pressure cook on HIGH for 5 minutes. Let the pressure drop NATURALLY for 15 minutes. Release any residual pressure with the QUICK-RELEASE method and carefully remove the lid. Drain and set the chickpeas aside.

2. Pre-heat the pressure cooker using the BROWN setting.

3. Add the oil and butter and cook the onion, garlic and saffron threads until the onion starts to become tender – about 5 minutes. Add the rice and stir well. Return the chickpeas to the cooker, pour in the water, season with the salt and pepper and lock the lid in place.

4. Pressure cook on HIGH for 6 minutes.

5. Release the pressure using the QUICK-RELEASE method and carefully remove the lid. Fluff the rice and chickpeas with a fork, mixing in the cilantro or parsley and transfer to a serving dish.

 Shortcut

Though I think cooking your chickpeas from their dried form is so much tastier, if you're in a hurry, use a can of chickpeas in this recipe. Drain and rinse the chickpeas and then add them to the cooker and cook them with the rice.

White Beans with Pancetta and Kale

You don't have to use the pancetta in this recipe, but it does add a nice saltiness to the beans. To make these beans a vegetarian option, simply omit the pancetta, substitute vegetable stock for the chicken stock, and drizzle a little olive oil onto the beans at the end.

Serves
6 to 8

Cooking Time
5 + 15 Minutes

Release Method
Natural-release

2 cups dried white beans

8 slices pancetta (or 6 slices bacon), sliced into 1-inch pieces

2 cloves garlic, minced

1 bay leaf

1 teaspoon salt

1 quart chicken stock

salt and freshly ground black pepper

4 cups packed shredded kale

¼ cup grated Parmesan cheese

1. Place the white beans in the pressure cooker and cover with an inch of water. Pressure cook on HIGH for 5 minutes. Let the pressure drop NATURALLY and carefully remove the lid. Drain and set the beans aside.

2. Pre-heat the pressure cooker using the BROWN setting.

3. Add the pancetta and cook until almost crispy. Remove the pancetta from the cooker and set aside. Add the garlic to the cooker and cook for 30 seconds. Return the beans to the cooker and add the bay leaf, salt and chicken stock. Lock the lid in place.

4. Pressure cook on HIGH for 15 minutes.

5. Let the pressure drop NATURALLY and carefully remove the lid.

6. Season to taste with salt and pepper and stir in the kale. Bring the liquid to a simmer using the BROWN setting. Simmer for about 4 to 5 minutes or until the kale is tender and cooked. Stir the cooked pancetta back into the beans and transfer to a serving dish. Sprinkle with Parmesan cheese and serve.

If you can't find, or don't have any kale, substitute spinach and cook for just a minute before returning the pancetta and serving.

Ham and Cheddar Grits

I'm far from being a Southerner, but I have to admit that grits in the morning are satisfying and delicious, no matter how you dress them up. The nice thing about cooking them in a pressure cooker is that you don't have to stand over them stirring while they cook.

Serves
4

Cooking Time
10 Minutes

Release Method
Natural-release

2 tablespoons butter

4½ cups water

1 cup coarse corn grits (not the instant variety)

1 teaspoon salt

7-ounce ham steak, small dice

1½ cups grated Cheddar cheese

½ cup milk (optional)

freshly ground black pepper or crushed red pepper flakes

chopped fresh chives

1. Bring the butter and water to a boil in the pressure cooker using the BROWN setting.

2. Whisk in the grits and salt and continue to whisk for a full minute so that the grits have a moment to become suspended in the water rather than sinking to the bottom of the cooker. Lock the lid in place.

3. Pressure cook on HIGH for 10 minutes.

4. Let the pressure drop NATURALLY and carefully remove the lid. Stir in the ham and cheese and season to taste with salt and lots of freshly ground black pepper. Stir in the milk to thin the grits a little and cool them to an edible temperature. Sprinkle chives on top and serve.

Dress It Up

While the grits are cooking, sauté some shrimp (peeled, deveined and tails removed) in olive oil with garlic and crushed red pepper flakes. At the very end of cooking, add a pinch of smoked paprika and a squeeze of lemon. Top the finished grits with the shrimp and call it a meal!

Quinoa Rice with Almonds

Quinoa is actually a seed, rather than a grain. The great thing about quinoa is that it is super high in protein and fits into a gluten-free diet really well. You can use red or white quinoa in this dish, depending on the look you want at the end. I think the red quinoa is particularly pretty.

Serves
4

Cooking Time
6 Minutes

Release Method
Natural-release

2 tablespoons butter, divided

½ onion, finely chopped

1 clove garlic, smashed

1 cup basmati rice

½ cup quinoa, rinsed

2 teaspoons salt

freshly ground black pepper

2½ cups water

½ cup chopped toasted almonds

1. Pre-heat the pressure cooker using the BROWN setting.

2. Add 1 tablespoon of the butter and cook the onion and garlic until the onion starts to become tender – about 5 minutes. Stir in the rice, quinoa, salt and pepper. Add the water and lock the lid in place.

3. Pressure cook on HIGH for 6 minutes.

4. Let the pressure drop NATURALLY and carefully remove the lid. Fluff the rice with a fork, remove the garlic clove, stir in the remaining butter and toasted almonds and serve.

The butter in this recipe is there purely for flavor, so if you're trying to lighten up, just leave out the butter and consider a little drizzle of olive oil at the end.

Rice and Vegetable Pilaf

This is a quick and easy side dish that cooks up in no time. You can create variations on this recipe very easily too. Use two cups of any combination of vegetables, but make sure they are cut up small enough to cook in the same time the rice takes – 5 minutes.

Serves
4 to 6

Cooking Time
5 Minutes

Release Method
Quick-release

1 tablespoon olive oil

½ cup onion, finely chopped

1 cup long grain white rice

½ cup red pepper, finely chopped

½ cup yellow squash, finely chopped

1 cup frozen diced peas and carrots

1½ cups chicken stock

4 tablespoons butter

2 teaspoons dried parsley

1 teaspoon salt

freshly ground black pepper

1. Pre-heat the pressure cooker using the BROWN setting.

2. Add the oil to the cooker and cook the onion until it starts to brown. Add the rice and cook for another 2 minutes, stirring to coat the kernels in oil. Add the red pepper, yellow squash, peas, carrots, chicken stock, butter, parsley, salt and freshly ground black pepper, stirring to combine. Lock the lid in place.

3. Pressure cook on HIGH for 5 minutes.

4. Release the pressure using the QUICK-RELEASE method and carefully remove the lid. Fluff rice and vegetables with a fork and transfer to a serving dish.

Brown Rice Salad with Artichoke Hearts, Avocado and Pinenuts

This is another room temperature salad, which means that you can make it ahead of time and focus on the main meal at hand. Or, this could actually be a main course salad all by itself.

Serves
8 (or 4 people as a main meal)

Cooking Time
20 Minutes

Release Method
Natural-release

1 tablespoon olive oil

1 onion, finely chopped

2 cups brown rice

2 teaspoons salt

freshly ground black pepper

4 cups water or chicken stock

1 tablespoon rice wine vinegar

½ teaspoon honey

½ teaspoon salt

freshly ground black pepper

3 tablespoons extra virgin olive oil

1 (12-ounce) jar artichoke hearts in water, drained and quartered

1 avocado, diced

2 ribs celery, thinly sliced

6 radishes, sliced

1½ cups halved cherry tomatoes

⅓ cup toasted pinenuts

¾ cup fresh parsley leaves

¾ cup fresh basil leaves, shredded

1. Pre-heat the pressure cooker using the BROWN setting.

2. Add the oil and sauté the onion until it starts to become tender – about 5 minutes. Add the rice, salt and pepper, pour in the water or chicken stock and lock the lid in place.

3. Pressure cook on HIGH for 20 minutes.

4. While the rice is cooking, prepare the vinaigrette. In a small bowl, combine the vinegar, honey, salt and freshly ground black pepper. Whisk in the olive oil and set aside.

5. Let the pressure drop NATURALLY and carefully remove the lid. Transfer the rice to a large salad bowl and fluff with a wooden spoon as you add the vinaigrette. Let the dressed rice cool for about 10 minutes.

6. Add all the remaining ingredients to the salad bowl and toss. Season to taste with salt and pepper and serve.

Brown rice is simply whole grain rice that has only the hull removed, leaving the bran and germ (the most nutritious part of the grain) intact. The deterrent to cooking brown rice is that it usually takes about 40 minutes on the stovetop. The pressure cooker cuts that time in half. Getting healthy in half the time? I wish that applied to my time at the gym!

Baked Beans

These are NOT the same beans that you had out of a can as a kid! Though reminiscent of the canned version, making the beans from scratch results in beans that have a firmer texture and a sauce that is delicious and hard to resist.

Serves
6 to 8

Cooking Time
5 + 18 Minutes

Release Method
Natural-release

2 cups dried navy or white beans

½ pound bacon, chopped

1 onion, finely chopped

2 cloves garlic, minced

¼ cup molasses

¼ cup tomato paste

¼ cup brown sugar

2 tablespoons cider vinegar

1 teaspoon dry mustard powder

1 bay leaf

1 teaspoon salt

1. Place the navy beans in the pressure cooker and cover with an inch of water. Pressure cook on HIGH for 5 minutes. Let the pressure drop NATURALLY and carefully remove the lid. Drain and set the beans aside.

2. Pre-heat the pressure cooker using the BROWN setting.

3. Add the bacon and cook until almost crispy. Remove bacon pieces and set aside. Drain off all but 1 tablespoon of the bacon fat. Add the onion and garlic to the cooker and cook for 2 to 3 minutes. Add the remaining ingredients, stir well and return the beans to the cooker. Pour in enough water to just cover the beans (about 2 cups) and lock the lid in place.

4. Pressure cook on HIGH for 18 minutes.

5. Let the pressure drop NATURALLY and carefully remove the lid.

6. Season to taste again with salt and let the beans cool before serving with the reserved cooked bacon sprinkled on top. The beans will continue to absorb liquid and get thicker as they cool.

Did You Know...?

For a thicker consistency, remove a cup or two of the beans, purée them in a blender or food processor and stir them back into the beans.

Vegetable Side Dishes

Potato Gratin

Being able to make potato gratin in the pressure cooker is a huge time saver. The liquid quantity in this recipe is at a minimum, so make sure as little liquid evaporates from the cooker as possible before pressure is reached. Stick around the kitchen while the pressure cooker is coming to pressure and push down firmly on the lid if any steam escapes from around the lid in the process. That will quickly form the seal needed to build pressure retaining the liquid inside.

Serves
6 to 8

Cooking Time
6 Minutes

Release Method
Quick-release

2 tablespoons butter

1 onion, finely chopped

2 cloves garlic, minced

1 tablespoon fresh thyme leaves

1 cup chicken or vegetable stock

1 cup heavy cream

2 teaspoons salt

lots of freshly ground black pepper

2 to 3 large Russet potatoes, peeled and thinly sliced (about 1 to 1½ pounds)

1 tablespoon butter

1 cup panko breadcrumbs

½ cup grated Parmesan cheese

fresh thyme for garnish

1. Pre-heat the pressure cooker using the BROWN setting.

2. Add the butter to the cooker and sauté the onion until it starts to become tender – about 5 minutes. Add the garlic and thyme and cook for another minute. Turn the cooker off, stir in the stock and heavy cream and season with salt and freshly ground black pepper. Then, add the potatoes, separating the slices so they don't stick together and each slice gets evenly coated in the liquid. The top layer of potatoes should be just partially covered in liquid. Lock the lid in place.

3. Pressure cook on HIGH for 6 minutes.

4. While the potatoes are cooking, heat a skillet over medium-high heat. Add the butter and toast the breadcrumbs in the skillet, tossing regularly. Set aside.

5. Release the pressure using the QUICK-RELEASE method and carefully remove the lid. Sprinkle the Parmesan cheese over the top of the potatoes and let the gratin cool with the lid off. The cheese will melt and the potatoes will absorb more liquid. Serve the gratin out of the pressure cooker on to plates and top with the reserved toasted breadcrumbs and fresh thyme.

Turn this dish from Pommes Dauphinoise (the fancy French way of saying potato gratin) into Pommes Boulangères by using more stock instead of the heavy cream.

Parsnip, Pear and Rosemary Mash

If you don't like parsnips, this recipe might change your mind. The pear sweetens the parsnips so gently and the rosemary adds a nice herbaceous note. This is a great fresh alternative to mashed potatoes.

Serves
4

Cooking Time
4 Minutes

Release Method
Quick-release

1 pound parsnips, peeled and chopped

1 pear, peeled and chopped

1 sprig fresh rosemary

2 tablespoons butter

¼ cup heavy cream

salt and freshly ground black pepper

1 teaspoon finely chopped fresh rosemary

1. Add the parsnips, pear and rosemary sprig to the pressure cooker and add enough water to just cover the parsnips and pears and lock the lid in place.

2. Pressure cook on HIGH for 4 minutes.

3. Release the pressure using the QUICK-RELEASE method and carefully remove the lid. Drain the vegetables and return them to the warm pressure cooker, removing the rosemary sprig. Add the butter and cream, and mash the parsnips using a potato masher, a food mill or just smash them with a good wooden spoon. Season to taste with salt and freshly ground black pepper and serve with a little fresh rosemary.

The starches in parsnips convert to sugar in the cold. So, store your parsnips (dried of any moisture) in a plastic bag in the refrigerator crisper drawer. They should keep there for up to a month.

Green Beans and Carrots with Mustard Vinaigrette

This vinaigrette is very versatile and can be used on any number of vegetables from potatoes to asparagus. Dressing the vegetables while they are still warm allows them to absorb all the great flavors in the vinaigrette.

Serves
4

Cooking Time
3 Minutes

Release Method
Quick-release

½ pound green beans, trimmed

½ pound baby cut carrots, halved lengthwise

salt and freshly ground black pepper

half a lemon

For the dressing:

1 tablespoon finely chopped shallots

2 tablespoons white wine vinegar

2 teaspoons whole grain mustard

1 teaspoon lemon zest

salt and freshly ground black pepper

6 tablespoons extra virgin olive oil

2 tablespoons chopped fresh parsley or tarragon

1. Place a rack inside the pressure cooker. Place the carrots in a steamer basket and place the green beans on top. Season to taste with salt and freshly ground black pepper. Place the steamer insert on the rack in the pressure cooker and pour in 1 cup of water. Squeeze the lemon over the vegetables and lock the lid in place.

2. Pressure cook on HIGH for 3 minutes.

3. While the vegetables are cooking, make the vinaigrette. Whisk together the shallots, vinegar, mustard, lemon zest, salt and freshly ground black pepper. Whisk in the olive oil and add the parsley. Season to taste again with salt and pepper. (This will make more vinaigrette than you need, but it's a great dressing to have on hand for an easy salad, a piece of grilled fish, or many other vegetables.)

4. Release the pressure using the QUICK-RELEASE method and carefully remove the lid. Remove steamer basket with oven mitts or tongs and transfer the vegetables to a serving bowl or plate. Dress the vegetables with the vinaigrette while they are still warm.

It's much easier to zest a whole lemon than to zest half a lemon. A whole lemon gives you something to hold on to while you're zesting, without juice spilling all over your hand. So, when making this recipe, try to remember to zest the lemon for the dressing first. THEN cut it in half to squeeze over the vegetables.

Brussels Sprouts with Bacon and Parmesan Cheese

Though Brussels sprouts may be one of the least popular vegetables in America, they might be hard to pass up with bacon and Parmesan cheese mixed in!

Serves
6

Cooking Time
6 Minutes

Release Method
Quick-release

5 slices bacon, chopped

1 pound Brussels sprouts, trimmed and halved

¼ cup shaved Parmesan cheese

1. Pre-heat the pressure cooker using the BROWN setting.

2. Add the bacon and cook until crispy. Remove the bacon to a side dish and set aside. Wipe out the pressure cooker.

3. Place the Brussels sprouts into a steamer basket and lower the steamer basket into the pressure cooker. Add 2 cups of water to the cooker and lock the lid in place.

4. Pressure cook on HIGH for 6 minutes.

5. Reduce the pressure using the QUICK-RELEASE method and carefully open the lid.

6. Remove the Brussels sprouts and toss with the crispy bacon pieces and the shaved Parmesan cheese before serving.

Steamed Artichokes with Lemon Aïoli

Artichokes come in many different sizes. When choosing artichokes for this recipe, make sure whatever you buy will fit into your pressure cooker. Artichokes are fun to eat as you pull off each leaf, dip it in the aïoli and draw the base of the leaf through your teeth to scrape off the soft part of the leaf. Remember to put out a bowl for the discarded leaves.

Serves
2 to 4

Cooking Time
12 Minutes

Release Method
Quick-release

1 cup mayonnaise

1 large clove garlic, minced and mashed into a paste

1 tablespoon lemon zest

2 tablespoons lemon juice

1 tablespoon chopped fresh chives

salt and freshly ground black pepper

2 medium artichokes

1 lemon

4 or 5 sprigs fresh thyme

1. Make the aioli by mixing together the mayonnaise, mashed garlic, lemon zest and juice, chives, salt and pepper in a bowl.

2. Prepare the artichokes by cutting off the top inch of the prickly leaves, or if you're not bothered by the prickly leaves, leave the artichokes whole. Cut off the stem to create a flat base.

3. Place a rack in the pressure cooker and rest the artichokes on top of the rack. Squeeze the lemon juice all over the artichokes and drop the squeezed halves into the cooker around the artichokes along with the fresh thyme sprigs. Add 2 cups of water to the cooker and lock the lid in place.

4. Pressure cook on HIGH for 12 minutes.

5. Reduce the pressure using the QUICK-RELEASE method and carefully remove the lid.

6. Before you transfer the artichokes to a serving dish, invert them over the pressure cooker to allow any hot water to escape from between the leaves. Serve with the aioli.

Peak season for artichokes is from March to May. Squeeze the artichoke together when selecting – the leaves should squeak if it's ripe.

Beets and Potatoes with Bacon

The bright red color of this dish is striking and always gets noticed! The potatoes break down a little more than the beets do, which helps to bind this dish together. I love the smoky bacon flavor with the earthy beets, but if you want to make this vegetarian, just substitute 2 tablespoons of extra virgin olive oil.

Serves
4

Cooking Time
6 Minutes

Release Method
Quick-release

3 large beets, peeled and diced (½-inch dice) (about 5 cups)

2 large yellow potatoes, scrubbed and diced (1-inch dice) (about 5 cups)

4 strips of bacon, chopped

1 red onion, finely chopped

½ cup heavy cream

¼ cup chopped fresh parsley

salt and freshly ground black pepper

1. Place the beets and potatoes into the pressure cooker and add enough water to just cover the vegetables. Lock the lid in place.

2. Pressure cook on HIGH for 6 minutes.

3. While the potatoes and beets are cooking, pre-heat a large skillet over medium-high heat. Add the bacon and cook for about 5 minutes. Add the onion and sauté with the bacon until the onion starts to become tender – another 5 minutes.

4. Release the pressure using the QUICK-RELEASE method and carefully remove the lid.

5. Drain the beets and potatoes and transfer to a large serving bowl. Add the bacon and onions and toss well. Stir in the heavy cream and parsley, season to taste with salt and freshly ground black pepper and serve.

 Shortcut

You can make this a one-pot dish if you cook the bacon and onion in the pressure cooker on the BROWN setting and set it aside before step 1, but then what would you do during the quick six minutes it takes for the vegetables to cook? 😊

Maque Choux

Maque Choux is a popular Creole dish from Louisiana that combines corn, bell peppers and in this version bacon and cream. It's sort of a cross between creamed corn and succotash.

Serves
4

Cooking Time
5 Minutes

Release Method
Quick-release

4 strips thick cut bacon, chopped

1 onion, chopped

1 clove garlic, minced

1 red bell pepper, chopped

1 green bell pepper, chopped

4 cups frozen corn kernels

1½ cups heavy cream

½ cup chicken stock

1 (14-ounce) can diced tomatoes, drained

½ teaspoon paprika

⅛ teaspoon cayenne pepper

½ teaspoon dried oregano

1 teaspoon salt

freshly ground black pepper

½ cup chopped scallions

1. Preheat the pressure cooker using the BROWN setting.

2. Add the bacon and cook until much of the fat has been rendered out, but it's not yet crispy. Add the onion and garlic and cook about 5 minutes until it starts to brown a little. Add the peppers, corn, heavy cream, chicken stock, tomatoes, paprika, cayenne pepper, oregano, salt and freshly ground black pepper, and lock the lid in place.

3. Pressure on HIGH for 5 minutes.

4. Release the pressure using the QUICK-RELEASE method and carefully remove lid. Stir in the scallions and serve.

You can definitely substitute fresh corn kernels for this dish, but add ½ cup of stock if you do.

Hasselback Potatoes
with Cheddar and Bacon

You can make two large potatoes with this method and then serve a half to each person. When cut in half, the potatoes reveal their delicious center and make quite an attractive presentation.

Serves
4

Cooking Time
35 to 40 Minutes

Release Method
Quick-release

½ pound bacon, diced

½ onion, finely chopped

4 small or 2 large baking potatoes

¼ cup butter, cut in small pieces

salt and freshly ground black pepper

1½ cups grated cheddar cheese

sour cream

scallions, sliced

1. Preheat the pressure cooker using the BORWN setting.

2. Add the bacon to the cooker and cook until much of the fat has rendered out, but it's not yet crispy. Add the onion and continue to cook until both the onion and bacon are browned. Remove the onion and bacon from cooker with a slotted spoon and drain on paper towels. Drain off any remaining grease and wipe the insert clean.

3. Slice six to eight slits across each potato parallel to the short ends of the potato, but only slice about three quarters of the way down, leaving the potato attached at the bottom. You should be able to just barely open the slits of the potato. Push a little piece of butter between each slice of potato, and top the butter with a spoonful of the bacon and onion mixture. Carefully open the pockets slightly to get filling inside, but don't worry if the potato breaks apart – you can always just push it back together when you wrap them in the next step.

4. Spray 2 or 4 large pieces of aluminum foil with cooking spray and place a potato on top of each one. Season well with salt and pepper and sprinkle the Cheddar cheese on each potato. Loosely wrap each potato with the aluminum foil by bringing 4 corners together above the potato and sealing tightly. The goal is to not have the foil touching the cheese.

5. Pour 1½ cups of water into the cooker. Place the potatoes on the rack (use a piece of crumpled up aluminum foil if you don't have a rack that fits your cooker). You can rest the potatoes on top of each other as necessary to fit in cooker, but try not to squish them.

6. Pressure cook on HIGH for 35 minutes for small potatoes, or 40 minutes for large potatoes.

7. Release the pressure using the QUICK-RELEASE method and carefully remove the lid. Transfer the potatoes to the counter and let them rest for a few minutes before unwrapping the aluminum foil. Top with the sour cream and scallions.

Corn on the Cob
with Sun-Dried Tomato and Basil Butter

Corn cooks very quickly in the pressure cooker and because it is steamed rather than boiled, it retains more of its nutrients this way. If you are using corn at peak season when it is super fresh, it will only need 2 minutes of cooking time. If the corn is out of season or a few days old, however, it will probably need another minute or two in the cooker.

Serves
4

Cooking Time
2 -3 Minutes

Release Method
Quick-release

¼ cup butter, softened

1 tablespoon chopped sun-dried tomatoes

1 tablespoons chopped fresh basil

salt and freshly ground black pepper

4 cobs of corn

1. Combine the softened butter with the sun-dried tomatoes and basil. This can be done by hand, or in a food processor. Season to taste with salt and pepper. Divide the butter into 8 equal portions. One easy way to do this is to roll the butter up in a piece of plastic wrap, twisting the ends to form a tube of butter, chill and when cool, cut into 8 pieces.

2. Place a rack or steamer basket into the pressure cooker. Add two cups of water to the cooker. Wrap each cob of corn with two pieces of the butter in aluminum foil, and place on the rack or steamer basket.

3. Pressure cook on HIGH for 2 to 3 minutes.

4. Reduce the pressure using the QUICK-RELEASE method and carefully remove the lid.

5. Unwrap the cobs of corn and serve, pouring the extra melted butter over the top and seasoning again with salt and freshly ground black pepper.

Did You Know...?

If you're making this compound butter, why not double the recipe and freeze what you have left over. It is delicious on grilled chicken or steak!

Sweet and Sour Red Cabbage

This dish is so vibrant in color and tangy in taste that it's sure to leave an impression! It's a tight fit for these ingredients in a four quart pressure cooker, but don't worry, the cabbage will wilt down in no time.

Serves
6 to 8

Cooking Time
5 Minutes

Release Method
Quick-release

1 tablespoon vegetable oil

1 red onion, sliced

2 pounds red cabbage, sliced (about 12 cups)

2 Granny Smith apples, peeled, cored and chopped

½ cup brown sugar

2 teaspoons caraway seeds

½ cup apple cider vinegar

½ cup balsamic vinegar

1 cup apple juice

salt and freshly ground black pepper

1. Pre-heat the pressure cooker using the BROWN setting.

2. Add the oil and cook the onion for a minute or two. Add the cabbage and apple and stir well. Combine the brown sugar, caraway seeds, apple cider vinegar, balsamic vinegar and apple juice, stir well and then pour the mixture over the cabbage. Lock the lid in place.

3. Pressure cook on HIGH for 5 minutes.

4. Reduce the pressure using the QUICK-RELEASE method and carefully remove the lid.

5. Season to taste with salt and pepper and transfer to a serving dish.

Dessert

Rum Raisin Rice Pudding

Caramel Pot de Crème

Quick and Easy Crème Brûlée

Reisling Poached Peaches

Banana Cake with Chocolate Chunks

Lemon Blueberry Cheesecake

Coconut Rice Pudding with Pineapple

Red Wine Blackberry Poached Pears

Strawberry Rhubarb Compote with Balsamic Vinegar

Chocolate Raspberry Almond Torte

Mint Chocolate Fudge Cake with Ganache

Rich Lemon Cake with Sugar Glaze

Rum Raisin Rice Pudding

This is like a warm version of rum raisin ice cream, which reminds me of my Dad since he used to love rum raisin ice cream when I was a kid. He also loves rice pudding, so this dessert is right up his alley!

Serves
6 to 8

Cooking Time
12 Minutes

Release Method
Quick-release

2 cups half and half

2 cups milk

1 tablespoon butter

½ cup sugar

1½ cups short-grain white rice
(like Arborio)

1 cinnamon stick

1 vanilla bean, split open
(or 2 teaspoons pure vanilla extract)

1 cup raisins

½ cup dark rum

1. Place all the ingredients except for the raisins and rum into the pressure cooker. Stir well to ensure that the vanilla seeds are dispersed throughout. Lock the lid in place.

2. Pressure cook on HIGH for 12 minutes. While the rice pudding is cooking, combine the raisins and rum in a small saucepan and bring to a boil. Simmer for a couple of minutes and then remove from the heat and set aside.

3. Release the pressure using the QUICK-RELEASE method and carefully remove the lid.

4. Remove the vanilla bean and the cinnamon stick pieces from the pudding. Stir in the rum and raisins and serve with more half and half if desired.

Thin leftover rice pudding with more milk or half and half. It will continue to get thicker as it sits in the fridge.

Caramel Pot de Crème

Oh boy! This dessert is a head-slapper! It's smooth, creamy and delicious. If you like caramel, you'll LOVE this. Just remember that pot de crèmes really do need some time to cool before serving. They are best made several hours or even a day before you need them.

Serves
4

Cooking Time
20 Minutes

Release Method
Quick-release

1½ cups sugar

¼ cup water

1 cup heavy cream

1 cup half and half

4 egg yolks

pinch salt

whipped cream (optional)

coarse sea salt (optional)

1. Combine the sugar and water in a saucepan. Over low heat, stir to dissolve the sugar. Increase the heat and bring the mixture to a boil. Stop stirring and instead swirl the pan every once in a while, as the sugar starts to brown and turn a deep amber color. Remove the pan from the heat and add the heavy cream and half and half. The mixture will bubble ferociously, but it will settle down and melt into a smooth liquid again when you return it to the heat. Stir over low heat until the caramel dissolves and then remove the pan from the heat.

2. In a separate bowl, beat the egg yolks until they are smooth and fall from the whisk like a ribbon. Whisk the warm caramel mixture into the egg yolks, adding the salt. (Should any of the egg form lumps, simply strain the mixture through a fine strainer.) Pour the mixture into 4 (6-ounce) ramekins and wrap each ramekin tightly in aluminum foil.

3. Pour enough water into the pressure cooker to cover the bottom by an inch. Place a rack in the bottom of the cooker and place the ramekins on the rack, stacking them on top of each other if necessary. Lock the lid in place.

4. Pressure cook on HIGH for 20 minutes.

5. Release the pressure using the QUICK-RELEASE method and carefully remove the lid.

6. Remove the ramekins from the cooker and unwrap them. They should still jiggle in the center. Cool at room temperature and then wrap with plastic wrap and refrigerate. Serve cold with a dollop of whipped cream, and a sprinkling of coarse sea salt if desired.

Quick and Easy Crème Brûlée

This dish has a fancy name and a certain level of intimidation to home cooks, but it's really not a difficult dessert to make. If you have a brûlée torch, it's that much easier to burn the sugar at the end, but you can make it work with your broiler too.

Serves
4

Cooking Time
6 Minutes

Release Method
Natural-release

5 egg yolks

¼ cup sugar

1½ cups heavy cream

1 teaspoon pure vanilla extract

pinch of salt

4 tablespoons sugar

1. In medium bowl, whisk the egg yolks and sugar together until fluffy and a light yellow color. Add the heavy cream and mix well. Stir in the vanilla extract and pinch of salt. Divide this mixture between 4 (6-ounce) ramekins. Wrap each ramekin in aluminum foil.

2. Pour 1½ cups of water into the pressure cooker. Place a rack or some crumpled up aluminum foil in the bottom of the cooker and stack the ramekins on the rack.

3. Pressure cook on HIGH for 6 minutes.

4. Let the pressure drop NATURALLY and carefully remove the lid. Let the ramekins cool a little on the counter and then refrigerate them for at least one hour until they are properly cooled and set.

5. Before serving, make the caramelized sugar topping by sprinkling one tablespoon of sugar on top of each ramekin. Using a brûlée torch, hold the flame about 2 inches from the ramekin and melt the sugar to form a light brown, hard topping. (If you don't have a brûlée torch, you can place the ramekins on a cookie sheet under the broiler for about 3 minutes, keeping you eyes on them so they don't burn.) Let the sugar set and harden a few minutes before serving.

Reisling Poached Peaches

This dessert really couldn't be simpler. Poaching fruit in a sweet wine just enhances the delicious fruit flavor, even with one minute of time under pressure. You could opt to peel the peaches first, but why bother when it's so easy to slip the skins off after poaching. This is best with peaches that are just ripe, but if your peaches are a little under-ripe, add a minute to the cooking time.

Serves
4

Cooking Time
1 Minute

Release Method
Quick-release

2 cups sweet Reisling white wine

1 cinnamon stick

¼ to ½ cup brown sugar

1 vanilla bean, split

4 peaches, cut in half and pit removed

1. Combine the wine, cinnamon, ¼ cup of the sugar and vanilla bean in the pressure cooker and taste it for sweetness. How much sugar you add will depend on the sweetness of the wine and the ripeness of the peaches. Add more sugar if you feel it needs more. Bring the mixture to a simmer using the BROWN setting. Stir to dissolve the sugar.

2. Add the peaches and lock the lid in place.

3. Pressure cook on HIGH for 1 minute.

4. Release the pressure using the QUICK-RELEASE method and carefully remove the lid.

5. Remove the peaches from the cooker using a slotted spoon and set aside to cool. At this point, you can easily slip off the skins of the peaches, but I think they add a nice color to the dish. Reduce the poaching liquid by simmering it using the BROWN setting. When the liquid has reached a syrupy consistency, remove, cool and combine with the poached fruit. Serve over ice cream, cheesecake or pie.

Banana Cake with Chocolate Chunks

Making cakes in the pressure cooker doesn't always speed up the time it takes to bake them, but it certainly keeps the cakes moist and delicious. The layers of chocolate in the center and on the top of this cake really make this cake look decadent, and in this case, looks are NOT deceiving!

Serves
6 to 8

Cooking Time
50 Minutes

Release Method
Natural-release

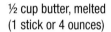

½ cup butter, melted
(1 stick or 4 ounces)

1 cup granulated sugar

1 egg

1 teaspoon pure vanilla extract

4 ripe bananas, mashed (about 1 cup)

½ cup sour cream

1 teaspoon baking soda

1½ cups all-purpose flour

1 teaspoon baking powder

¼ teaspoon salt

1 cup semi-sweet or bitter-sweet chocolate chunks

¼ cup brown sugar

¼ teaspoon ground cinnamon

1. Butter a 7-inch cake pan.

2. Mix the melted butter, sugar, egg, vanilla extract and bananas together in a large bowl. In a second bowl, combine the sour cream and the baking soda. In a third bowl, combine the flour, baking powder and salt. Finally, in a fourth bowl, combine the chocolate chunks, brown sugar and cinnamon. Add the flour mixture to the butter mixture, alternating with the sour cream mixture. Pour half of the batter into the buttered cake pan. Scatter half of the chocolate chip mixture on top. Cover with the remaining batter and then sprinkle the remaining chocolate chip mixture on top. Wrap the pan completely in a piece of well-greased aluminum foil.

3. Place a rack in the bottom of the pressure cooker and add 2 cups of water. Lower the cake pan into the cooker using a sling made of aluminum foil (fold a piece of aluminum foil into a strip about 2-inches wide by 24-inches long). Fold the ends of the aluminum foil into the cooker and lock the lid in place.

4. Pressure cook on HIGH for 50 minutes. (If you are using a silicone cake pan, increase this time to 60 minutes.)

5. Let the pressure drop NATURALLY and carefully remove the lid. Remove the cake pan from the cooker and let it cool. Transfer the cake to a serving plate and serve with a dollop of whipped cream if desired.

Shortcut

If you're craving banana cake RIGHT NOW, and don't have any bananas on hand, all is not lost! You can speed-ripen your bananas by popping them into a 300°F oven for 30 to 40 minutes (still in their peels). Line the baking sheet with some parchment first – the bananas have a tendency to leak a little as they "ripen".

Lemon Blueberry Cheesecake

This cheesecake has a bright lemony flavor that contrasts nicely with the sweet and creamy cheese. Remember, a cheesecake needs time to set up after cooking – at least 8 hours – so this is a dessert that you need to make for tomorrow, not today.

Serves
6 (makes one 7-inch cheesecake)

Cooking Time
22 Minutes + 8 Hours to cool

Release Method
Natural-release

6 graham crackers, crushed

1 teaspoon finely grated lemon zest

2 tablespoons butter, melted

1 cup fresh or frozen blueberries, plus more for garnish

1 to 2 tablespoons sugar (depending on the sweetness of the blueberries)

1 teaspoon cornstarch

Juice of ½ a lemon

16 ounces (1 pound) cream cheese, room temperature

⅔ cup sugar

1 tablespoon lemon juice

2 teaspoons finely grated lemon zest

2 eggs

1. Line the inside of a 7-inch cake pan with a large piece of greased aluminum foil (greased side facing up), pushing it into all the edges of the pan.

2. Crush the graham crackers and the lemon zest together in a food processor until they form fine crumbs. Mix the crumbs with the butter and press the crumb mixture into the base of the cake pan. Refrigerate while you prepare the cheesecake batter.

3. Place the blueberries, sugar, cornstarch and juice of half a lemon in a small saucepan and bring to a boil. Stir, crushing the blueberries as you go, and simmer until the sauce has thickened slightly. Let the blueberries cool and then transfer them to a zipper sealable bag.

4. Using the paddle on your stand mixer with low speed, or the regular beaters on a hand mixer on low speed, or a food processor (scraping the sides of the processor bowl several times) blend the cream cheese until it is completely smooth with no lumps. When all the lumps in the cream cheese have disappeared, add the sugar, lemon juice and lemon zest. Blend to incorporate the ingredients and then add the eggs one at a time, mixing only to distribute the eggs evenly in the batter. Do not over-mix at this point.

5. Pour half the batter into the cake pan with the graham cracker crust. Cut a corner off the zipper sealable bag with the blueberry mixture and drizzle half the blueberry mixture over the cheesecake in a zigzag pattern. Run a knife through the sauce, perpendicular to the zigzags to create a swirl look. Repeat with the remaining cheesecake batter and blueberries, making a pretty swirl pattern on top. Cover the pan tightly with more greased aluminum foil.

6. Place a rack in the bottom of the pressure cooker and add 2 cups of water. Lower the cake pan into the cooker using a sling made of aluminum foil (fold a piece of aluminum foil into a strip about 2-inches wide by 24-inches long). Fold the ends of the aluminum foil into the cooker and lock the lid in place.

7. Pressure cook on HIGH for 22 minutes. (if you are using a silicon cake pan, increase the time to 30 minutes.)

8. Let the pressure drop NATURALLY and let the cheesecake sit in the turned off pressure cooker for one hour. Carefully remove the lid and transfer the cheesecake from the cooker to the counter using the aluminum sling or rack. Let the cheesecake come to room temperature and then remove the foil from the top of the cake pan. Blot any liquid that might have condensed on the surface of the cake, wrap it in plastic wrap and refrigerate for at least 8 hours.

9. Bring the cake to room temperature before serving, and serve with more fresh blueberries and lemon zest if desired.

Coconut Rice Pudding with Pineapple

When you want to feel like you're in the tropics, this is the ticket! Instead of pineapple, try topping it with mango and strawberries for a change.

Serves
6 to 8

Cooking Time
12 Minutes

Release Method
Quick-release

1 (14 ounce) can coconut milk

2 cups half and half

1 cup whole milk

1 tablespoon butter

½ cup sugar

1½ cups short-grain white rice

1 cinnamon stick

⅛ teaspoon grated nutmeg

1 vanilla bean, split open OR
2 teaspoons pure vanilla extract

½ cup toasted shredded coconut

1 cup pineapple chunks

1. Place all the ingredients except the shredded coconut and pineapple into the pressure cooker. Stir well and lock the lid in place.

2. Pressure cook on HIGH for 12 minutes.

3. Release the pressure using the QUICK-RELEASE method and carefully remove the lid.

4. Stir the pudding and then let it sit for 5 minutes – it will thicken up as it sits. Garnish the pudding with the toasted coconut and pineapple chunks.

Use a dry skillet to toast shredded coconut. Cook over medium heat, tossing regularly until the coconut is lightly browned. Remove immediately to a plate to avoid burning it.

Red Wine Blackberry Poached Pears

The blackberries in this recipe break down and become part of the sauce for the pears, almost as if you were using blackberry wine to poach the pears. It does take some time at the end to really reduce the cooking liquid into a delectable sauce for the pears, but it's worth it so try to be patient.

Serves
4

Cooking Time
5 to 7 Minutes

Release Method
Natural-release

1 bottle red wine

1 cinnamon stick

3 cloves

¾ cup sugar

4 strips orange peel, 3-inch long

2 cups blackberries

4 pears, peeled, sliced in half and the seeds removed with a teaspoon

basil or mint leaves, for garnish

1. Combine the red wine, cinnamon stick, cloves, sugar, orange peel and blackberries in the pressure cooker.

2. Place the pears in the liquid and lock the lid in place.

3. Pressure cook on HIGH for 5 to 7 minutes, depending on the ripeness of the pears.

4. Let the pressure drop NATURALLY and carefully remove the lid. Remove the pears and set aside to cool. Meanwhile, return the pressure cooker to the BROWN setting and reduce the sauce by two-thirds (this could take 30 minutes or so).

5. Serve the pear halves with the syrup poured over the top and garnish with either a basil or mint leaf next to the stem.

Strawberry Rhubarb Compote with Balsamic Vinegar

While this is not the prettiest of compotes, it is super delicious! You can serve it over a variety of desserts from vanilla ice cream, to cheesecake to just a piece of cake, or use it as the base for a strawberry rhubarb crumble or pie.

Serves
1 Quart

Cooking Time
3 Minutes

Release Method
Natural-release

2 pounds rhubarb, chopped into 1-inch pieces (about 6 cups)

1 pound fresh strawberries, hulled and left whole (about 3 cups)

1 cup granulated sugar

1 cup apple cider

½ cup water

⅛ teaspoon salt

2 tablespoons balsamic vinegar

1. Combine all the ingredients except for the balsamic vinegar in the pressure cooker. Lock the lid in place.

2. Pressure cook on HIGH for 3 minutes.

3. Let the pressure drop NATURALLY and carefully remove the lid.

4. Transfer the fruit to a bowl with a slotted spoon and cool to room temperature. Add some of the cooking liquid to the fruit – just enough to bring the compote to the desired consistency. Stir in the balsamic vinegar and serve warm or cool over ice cream, cheesecake or pie.

Rhubarb season starts early in April or May and goes through to the fall. Interestingly, the leaves of rhubarb are toxic, which is why you only see the stalks for sale in grocery stores.

Chocolate Raspberry Almond Torte

This almost flourless torte is not dense, but light in texture and not overly sweet. With a dollop of whipped cream it makes a nice, civilized, but decadent dessert.

Serves
6 to 8

Cooking Time
30 Minutes

Release Method
Combo

6 ounces semi-sweet chocolate, chopped

½ cup butter

3 eggs

½ teaspoon pure vanilla extract

⅓ cup sugar

¼ cup all-purpose flour

1 cup frozen raspberries, defrosted and drained

toasted sliced almonds, fresh raspberries, powdered sugar and heavy cream, for serving

1. Butter a 7-inch cake pan.

2. Melt the chocolate and butter together, either in the microwave or in a double boiler.

3. In a separate bowl, beat the eggs vigorously until they are thick and fall from the beater in one solid line like a ribbon. Whisk the vanilla extract and sugar into the eggs. Drizzle in the chocolate and butter, mixing well. Stir in the flour, combining until there are no lumps. Finally, fold in the raspberries. Pour the batter into the buttered cake pan and then wrap the pan completely in buttered aluminum foil.

4. Place a rack in the bottom of the pressure cooker and add 2 cups of water. Lower the cake pan into the cooker using a sling made of aluminum foil (fold a piece of aluminum foil into a strip about 2-inches wide by 24-inches long). Fold the ends of the aluminum foil into the cooker and lock the lid in place.

5. Pressure cook on HIGH for 30 minutes. (If you are using a silicon cale pan, increase the time to 35 minutes.)

6. Let the pressure drop NATURALLY for 10 minutes. Then, release any residual pressure using the QUICK-RELEASE method and carefully remove the lid. Remove the cake pan from the cooker and let it cool. Invert the cake onto a serving plate. Sprinkle the toasted almonds, fresh raspberries and powdered sugar on top and serve with a dollop of whipped cream.

Mix a little crème fraîche into your heavy cream for a whipped topping that won't deflate over time. Crème fraîche is a soured cream that you can find in specialty dairy sections, and its high butterfat content (higher than heavy cream) helps to hold the whipped air pockets in whipped cream. It also has a nice tang to it that really compliments the chocolate raspberry almond torte.

Mint Chocolate Fudge Cake with Ganache

The pressure cooker gives this cake a dense fudgy texture, which is a nice contrast to the light mint flavor in the cake and ganache. It's a hard one to turn down!

Serves
8

Cooking Time
60 Minutes

Release Method
Natural-release

1 box chocolate cake mix

1 (4.5-ounce) box instant chocolate pudding

1 cup hot water

¾ cup butter, melted

3 eggs

1 cup crème de menthe chocolate pieces (such as Andes®), chopped

½ cup heavy cream

1 cup mint chocolate chips

14 crème de menthe chocolate mint thins, broken into 3 pieces

1. In large bowl, mix the chocolate cake mix, instant pudding, hot water, melted butter and eggs together until combined and smooth. Fold in the crème de menthe candy pieces and transfer the batter to a greased 7-inch cake pan. Wrap the pan with aluminum foil, leaving a dome of aluminum foil on top of the cake pan to allow the batter to rise.

2. Place a rack in the bottom of the pressure cooker and add 2 cups of water. Lower the cake pan into the cooker using a sling made of aluminum foil (fold a piece of aluminum foil into a strip about 2 inches wide by 24 inches long). Fold the ends of the aluminum fold into the cooker and lock the lid into place.

3. Pressure cook on HIGH for 60 minutes.

4. Let the pressure drop NATURALLY and carefully remove the lid. Remove the cake pan from the cooker and let it cool. Once the cake pan is cool, remove the cake from the pan and place on a cooling rack over a cookie sheet.

5. To make the ganache, heat the heavy cream in a small saucepan until it simmers, but do not let it boil. Place the mint chocolate chips in a large bowl and pour the warm cream over the top. Stir until chocolate chips are melted and smooth. Let the ganache sit for 3 minutes. Then, slowly pour the ganache onto the middle of the cake and spread it in a circular motion to cover the top of the cake. Let the ganache drip down the sides of the cake. You can either leave the drips of ganache down sides of the cake, or smooth it out by running a knife around the sides to completely cover the cake. If you need to, you can re-use the ganache that falls off the cake onto the cookie sheet to cover any spaces. Garnish the top of the cake with the broken crème de menthe mints and let it sit at room temperature until the ganache has set before serving.

If you want to go hog wild on decorating this cake, melt ½ cup of white chocolate chips with 1 tablespoon of heavy cream in the microwave for 30 seconds. Stir until the mixture is smooth and add a couple drops of green food coloring so the chocolate is a light green color. Drizzle lines of the white (now green) chocolate across the top of the cake and run a wooden skewer or thin knife through the lines in the opposite direction.

Rich Lemon Cake with Sugar Glaze

If you like lemon, you'll love this cake. Because it bakes in such a moist environment, it has a more dense texture than most cakes, which enhances the lemon flavor. The crumb topping that you put on top doesn't stay in crumb form, but melts into a sugary crust on top of the cake. If you have a sweet tooth, this cake's for you!

Serves
8

Cooking Time
55 Minutes

Release Method
Natural-release

1 box butter recipe vanilla cake mix

1 (4.5-ounce) box instant lemon pudding

1 cup water

½ cup butter, melted

3 eggs

zest of 2 lemons

¼ cup fresh lemon juice

½ cup flour

⅓ cup sugar

¼ cup melted butter

¾ cup powdered sugar

1 to 3 tablespoons fresh lemon juice

1. In large bowl, mix the cake mix, instant pudding, water, the ½ cup of melted butter and eggs together until combined and smooth. Stir in the lemon zest and juice. Transfer the batter to a greased 7-inch cake pan.

2. Mix the flour, sugar and ¼ cup of melted butter in a small bowl with a fork to form coarse crumbs. Sprinkle this mixture evenly over the top of the cake. Wrap the pan with aluminum foil, leaving a dome of foil on the top to allow the batter to rise.

3. Place on a rack in the bottom of the pressure cooker and add 2 cups of water. Lower the cake pan into the cooker using a sling made of aluminum foil (fold a piece of aluminum foil into a strip about 2 inches wide by 24 inches long). Fold the ends of the aluminum foil into the cooker and lock the lid into place.

4. Pressure on HIGH for 55 minutes.

5. Let the pressure drop NATURALLY and carefully remove the lid. Remove the cake pan from the cooker and let it cool for 10 minutes. Then, carefully remove the cake from the pan and place it on cooling rack. The cake will naturally sink a little in the middle.

6. When cake is has cooled, whisk the confectionary sugar and 1 tablespoon of the lemon juice together until smooth. Add more lemon juice, a little at a time until the glaze has a thick but pourable consistency. Drizzle the glaze over the top of the cake in opposite directions, letting it drip down the sides. (If you find the glaze is getting absorbed into the cake, add a little more powdered sugar to make it thicker.) Garnish with 3 half moon slices of fresh lemon placed in the middle of the cake, where it has a tendency to sink a little.

Index

Index

Index

Index

Index

Index

Index

Notes

Cooking Charts

	Cooking Time HIGH pressure (minutes)	Liquid Needed	Release Method		Cooking Time HIGH pressure (minutes)	Liquid Needed	Release Method
Poultry							
Chicken Bones for stock	40	6 cups	NATURAL	Chicken Thigh (boneless)	4	1 cup	QUICK
Chicken Breast (bone in)	6	1 cup	QUICK	Chicken, Whole	20	1½ cups	NATURAL
Chicken Breast (boneless)	4	1 cup	QUICK	Cornish Game Hen (1 to 1½ pounds)	8	1 cup	NATURAL
Chicken Thigh (bone in)	7	1 cup	QUICK	Turkey Breast (boneless, 2 to 3 pounds)	20 to 25	1½ cups	NATURAL
Beef							
Beef Bones for stock	40	6 cups	NATURAL	Meatloaf	35	1½ cups	NATURAL
Brisket (3½ to 4 pounds)	55 to 65	1½ cups	NATURAL	Pot Roast (3½ to 4 pounds)	55 to 65	2 cups	NATURAL
Corned Beef Brisket	55	covered	NATURAL	Short Ribs	55	1½ cups	NATURAL
Flank Steak (1 pound)	25	1 cup	NATURAL	Stew Meat (1-inch cubes)	15 to 20	1 cup	NATURAL
Ground Beef	5	1 cup	QUICK	Veal Shanks	20 to 25	1½ cups	NATURAL
Meatballs	5	1 cup	NATURAL	Veal Stew Meat (1-inch cubes)	10	1 cup	NATURAL
Pork							
Baby Back Ribs	30	1 cup	NATURAL	Pork Chops (boneless, 1-inch)	4 to 5	1½ cups	NATURAL
Country Style Ribs	20 to 25	1½ cups	NATURAL	Pork Loin (2 to 2½ pounds)	25	1½ cups	NATURAL
Ground Pork	5	1 cup	QUICK	Pork Shoulder (3 pounds)	55	1½ cups	NATURAL
Ham (bone in, 5 pounds, pre-cooked)	25 to 30	1½ cups	NATURAL	Sausages	10 to 15	1½ cups	QUICK
Meatballs	5	1 cup	NATURAL	Spare Ribs	45	1 cup	NATURAL
Pork Chops (bone in, 1-inch)	6	1½ cups	NATURAL	Stew Meat (1-inch cubes)	15 to 20	1 cup	NATURAL
Lamb							
Ground Lamb	5	1 cup	QUICK	Leg of Lamb (boneless, 3½ to 4 pounds)	35 to 45	1½ cups	NATURAL
Lamb Shanks	30	1½ cups	NATURAL	Stew Meat (1-inch cubes)	15 to 20	1 cup	NATURAL
Meatballs	5	1 cup	NATURAL				
Fish and Seafood							
Calamari	20	5 cup	QUICK	Mussels	4	2 cup	QUICK
Clams	4	1 cup	QUICK	Salmon	5	4 cup	QUICK
Crab Legs	4	1 cup	QUICK	Shrimp	2	3 cup	QUICK
Fish Fillet (1-inch thick)	5	6 cup	QUICK				

Cooking Charts

Grains (1 cup)

	Cooking Time HIGH pressure (minutes)	Liquid Needed	Release Method
Barley (pearled)	20 to 25	3 cups	QUICK
Brown Rice	20	2 cups	NATURAL
Bulgur	6	2 cups	QUICK
Farro (pearled)	8	2 cups	QUICK
Farro (whole grain)	18	3 cups	QUICK
Polenta (coarse, not instant)	8 to 10	4 cups	QUICK
Poletna (fine, not instant)	5	4 cups	QUICK
Quinoa	5	1½ cups	QUICK
Steel Cut Oats	5	3 cups	NATURAL
White Rice, long-grain	4 to 6	1½ cups	QUICK
White Rice, short-grain	7	2⅔ cups	QUICK
Wild Rice	22	3 to 4 cups	QUICK

Beans and Legumes

	Un-Soaked	Soaked or Quick-Soaked	Release Method
Black Beans	25	7	NATURAL
Black-Eyed Peas	8	6	NATURAL
Cannellini Beans	25	7	NATURAL
Chickpeas	35 to 40	15	NATURAL
Great Northern Beans	25	8 to 10	NATURAL
Kidney Beans	25	8 to 10	NATURAL
Lentils	7 to 8	unnecessary	QUICK
Navy Beans	20	8 to 10	NATURAL
Pinto Beans	25	8 to 10	NATURAL
Split Peas	8 to 10	unnecessary	NATURAL
White Beans	20	8 to 10	NATURAL

Vegetables

	Cooking Time HIGH pressure (minutes)	Liquid Needed	Release Method
Acorn Squash (halved)	8	1 cup	QUICK
Artichokes (medium, whole)	12	1 cup	QUICK
Asparagus	2	1 cup	QUICK
Beets (medium, whole)	15	1 cup	QUICK
Broccoli	3	1 cup	QUICK
Broccoli Rabe	3	1 cup	QUICK
Brussels Sprouts	4 to 6	1 cup	QUICK
Butternut Squash (1-inch cubes)	5	1 cup	QUICK
Cabbage (quartered)	4 to 6	1 cup	QUICK
Beets (medium, whole)	15	1 cup	QUICK
Cauliflower (whole)	12 to 15	1 cup	QUICK
Collard Greens	5 to 10	1 cup	QUICK
Corn on the Cob	2 to 3	1 cup	QUICK
Eggplant	3 to 4	1 cup	QUICK
Fennel (wedges)	4	1 cup	QUICK
Green Beans	3 to 4	1 cup	QUICK
Kale	4	1 cup	QUICK
Leeks (1-inch pieces)	4	1 cup	QUICK
Parsnips (1-inch chunks)	4 to 5	1 cup	QUICK
Potatoes (1-inch chunks or small whole)	6 to 8	1 cup	QUICK
Rutabaga (1-inch chunks)	4	1 cup	QUICK
Spaghetti Squash (halved)	12 to 15	1 cup	QUICK
Sweet Potatoes (1-inch chunks)	4 to 5	1 cup	QUICK
Swiss Chard	2	1 cup	QUICK
Turnips (1-inch chunks)	3 to 4	1 cup	QUICK

Notes